Chinese American Poetry:
An Anthology

Chinese American Poetry: An Anthology

Edited by L. Ling-chi Wang
and Henry Yiheng Zhao

Assisted by Carrie L. Waara
Foreword by Sucheng Chan

Asian American Voices
Santa Barbara

Distributed by
University of Washington Press
Seattle and London

Copyright © 1991 by L. Ling-chi Wang and Henry Yiheng Zhao

Published by
Asian American Voices

Distributed by
The University of Washington Press,
PO Box 50096,
Seattle, Washington,
98145-5096

Printed in the United States of America

Library of Congress Cataloging in Publication Data

Chinese American poetry: an anthology / edited by L. Ling-chi Wang
   and Henry Yiheng Zhao, assisted by Carrie Waara ; foreword by
   Sucheng Chan.
      p.   cm.
   ISBN 0-295-97154-1 (pbk.)
      1. American poetry--Chinese American authors. 2. Chinese
   Americans--Poetry.   I. Wang, L. Ling-chih, 1938-   II. Chao, I-heng.
   III. Waara, Carrie L.
   PS591.C48A5 1991
   811' .54080951--dc20
                                                      91-19091
                                                      CIP

The copyright to the poems is held by the individual poets with the following exceptions:
   "Dreaming of Hair," "Early in the Morning," "My Indigo," "I Ask My Mother to Sing," "Ash, Snow or Moonlight," and "Visions and Interpretations" by Li-Young Lee first appeared in *Rose*, copyright © 1986 by Boa Editions, Ltd. Reprinted by permission of the Editor.
   "Living Conditions" by Russell Leong first appeared in *Frontiers of Asian American Studies*, © 1989 by Washington State University Press. Reprinted by permission.
   "My Father's Martial Art" by Stephen Liu first appeared in the *Antioch Review*, Vol. 39, No. 3 (Summer, 1981). Copyright © 1981 by The Antioch Review, Inc. Reprinted by permission.

Requests for permission to reprint should be addressed to:
Asian American Voices, c/o Asian American Studies Program
University of California, Santa Barbara, CA 93106

Contents

Foreword

Getting this anthology published has been a collective enterprise. It was conceived by Ling-chi Wang and Henry Yiheng Zhao in the mid-1980s. Their goal was to compile a bilingual volume of poems by Chinese Americans—individuals of Chinese ancestry now living in the United States and writing and publishing works in English. They contacted every Chinese American poet they could think of and asked each to send a portfolio of the poems, published and unpublished, that he or she wished to have considered. Out of the materials they received, the editors chose 162 poems for inclusion.

Only after making the selections did they turn to the task of finding a publisher, but none seemed interested in producing a bilingual text. Zhao, who is from the People's Republic of China and who translated the poems from English to Chinese in consultation with Sau-ling Wong, eventually persuaded Shanghai Wenyi Chubanshe (Shanghai Literature and Art Publishers) to print the Chinese version, which appeared in 1990. The Chinese edition is entitled *The Intention of Two Rivers*, a phrase borrowed from Mei-mei Berssenbrugge and rendered as *Liangtiao he di yitu* in Chinese. The Chinese and English versions of the anthology do not contain the same number of poems, however. For reasons of economy, the former includes only about one-third of the poems found here.

While the Chinese edition was in press, Zhao received his Ph.D., found a teaching job in England, and left the country. Wang, meanwhile, became too preoccupied with other responsibilities to take care of the details required to get an English edition published. He asked me if I would be willing to complete the project that he and Zhao had initiated. I agreed to do so, as all the poems had already been chosen and the introduction had been written. All that was left to do was to check who owned the copyright for each poem, obtain permission to reprint, produce camera-ready copy for the entire anthology, and find a publisher and distributor. I was lucky to have a patient and dedicated assistant, Carrie L. Waara, who took care of many of these details.

Though literature is not my field, I felt it was imperative to bring closure to the project because we have an obligation to the poets who have so generously contributed their writings to make this compilation possible. Moreover, I believe this collection has an importance that transcends poetry *per se*.

As a historian, I am painfully aware of the many gaps that exist in our knowledge of Asian American history. The Chinese and other Asian immigrants who came to America in the nineteenth and early twentieth centuries left fewer written records than did most European immigrant groups. The Asian immigrants' struggle for survival in a hostile environment, as well as cataclysmic events beyond their control, account for the paucity of materials. Large numbers of the first wave of immigrants—be they Chinese, Japanese, Koreans, Filipinos, or Indians —managed to find only seasonal work that forced them to live as migrant laborers. Some were illiterate, but even those who were not found little time to write. Some who did write had no permanent homes in which their manuscripts could be safely kept.

In the case of the Chinese, though they used professional letter writers to send missives home, not a great deal of what was mailed to China has been preserved, as war and revolution ravaged that country virtually without pause for more than a century. In the United States, the fire that accompanied the 1906 earthquake in San Francisco demolished that city's Chinatown, so all written records then in existence went up in flames. Most of the extant Chinese-language sources (many listed by Him Mark Lai in *A History Reclaimed: An Annotated Bibliography of Chinese Language Materials on the Chinese of America*, 1988) are organizational, and not personal, records. While these will definitely enable scholars to produce a more multi-dimensional history—one that reflects Chinese American perspectives —they do not necessarily tap at Chinese American sensibilities.

The Japanese left far more documents but these are also incomplete. After the United States declared war against Japan in December, 1941, agents from the Federal Bureau of Investigation picked up the most important leaders in the Japanese immigrant communities along the Pacific Coast and in Hawaii and interned them. Members of some families, fearful that Japanese-language writings and cultural artifacts might be used to incriminate them, purposely destroyed what documents, letters, and photographs they had in their possession. In short, Asian American history has been cruel to historiography.

Given this shortage of personal memorabilia, it is very difficult for historians of Asian America to reconstruct and depict the subjective consciousness of Asian immigrants. Joy, contentment, resignation, anguish, anger—all these, with rare exceptions, can only be inferred. Though there are some autobiographies, essays, and poems available, we can never be sure how representative they are. More has been left by the immigrants' children, some of whom were interviewed by, or who wrote autobiographies at the request of, social scientists in the 1920s, but these reflect the kind of information the scholars sought more than what the youngsters themselves felt and thought.

With the existence of such a vacuum, the creative writings of Asian American novelists, short story writers, playwrights, and poets take on added significance. Whether or not they wish to, Asian American writers and artists shoulder a special burden: the products of their imagination must often be used to flesh out the skeletal frames that historians and social scientists construct. This does not mean that "history" and "literature" are interchangeable or should be conflated; rather, they complement each other, each in its own way adding a few more strokes to the canvas. More so than for members of other ethnic groups, Asian American writers and artists must see forms and colors where others perceive only murky depths; they must sing of truths that others find inchoate.

When I was a child, many of the sing-song verses I wrote were published in school magazines. Ah, my teachers predicted, she will be a poet. But that was not to be. Though I still read poetry for solace, the more scholarly I became, the less poetry links me to sentient worlds within and beyond, for my mind now moves along a different plane. Perhaps my decision to complete the project that Ling-chi Wang and Henry Zhao started is a compensation of sorts for the poetic sensibility I lost so long ago.

Sucheng Chan

Santa Barbara, 1991

Acknowledgments

The people to whom we owe the most are the poets who contributed their work to this anthology. We are also deeply grateful to Sucheng Chan and Carrie L. Waara, who assumed responsibility for the production of this volume, and to Hung Liu, who generously allowed us to reproduce her painting, "Men and Elephant," on the cover of this book.

We also wish to acknowledge the pioneering role played by the following publications and publishers, who first introduced many of the poems included here to the American public: *Amerasia Journal; American Poetry Review; Antioch Review*; Asian Women United; Bamboo Ridge Press; Boa Editions, Ltd.; *boundary 2; Boxcar; Bridge*; Burning Deck; *Cincinnatti Poetry Review; Columbia: A Magazine of Poetry & Prose; Contact II*; Copper Canyon Press; Floating Island Publications; Great Raven Press; Greenfield Review Press; *Hapa*; Heinemann; Holt, Rinehart, Winston; *International Examiner*; Jordan Davis; *Journal of Ethnic Studies*; Lost Roads Publishers; *Milkweed Chronicle; Missouri Review; North Dakota Quarterly; Painted Bride Quarterly; Pembroke Magazine*; Radical Women Publications; Reed & Cannon; Sheep Meadow Press; *Sunbury Magazine; The Literary Review*; Tooth of Time Books; *University of Windsor Review; Village Voice; Virginia Quarterly Review*; Washington State University Press; West End Press; *Westerly; Wisconsin Review; Women's Review of Books*; and *World Englishes*.

Finally, we thank the Asian American Studies programs of the Berkeley and Santa Barbara campuses of the University of California for their financial support.

L.L.C.W and H.Y.Z.

xv

Introduction

Chinese American literature does not have a very long history. Most of the poets included in this anthology are rather young. Even those who have had a longer writing career—Diana Chang, Alan Lau, Alex Kuo, John Yau and some others—did not have their solo publications until the late 1970s. Not until the mid-1980s did a noticeable group of Chinese Americans producing good poetry appear. Their collective effort has become a sociocultural phenomenon that can no longer be ignored. In 1986 we decided to compile this anthology to record samples of their work.

Though the history of Chinese American literature is brief, Chinese living in the United States began to write in English almost a century ago. Sui Sin Far, an Eurasian born in England, began to publish short stories in the late nineteenth century, but she was an exceptional case.[1] A few other writers of Chinese ancestry, born and brought up in China but cast upon this land for various reasons, also published works in English. The earliest collection of poems in English seems to have been published by Moon Kwan, a student in Los Angeles.[2] The fall of the Qing Dynasty spurred Princess Der Ling to produce exotic novels about Manchu palace life, while the subsequent political turmoil turned the journalist H. T. Tsiang into a "proletarian" novelist who wrote about the 1911 Chinese revolution. The works of Lin Yutang, a Chinese writer extremely well-versed in English, won a broad readership in the 1940s. With a few exceptions, none of the works these writers produced, however, are about the Chinese-American experience *per se*.[3] Chinese American literature, in contrast, is the cultural expression of Chinese living in America. It is a part of the emerging ethnic minority literature of the United States.

In her 1984 bibliographic review of Asian American writers in *American Studies International*, Elaine Kim observed "a continual broadening" of contemporary Asian American creative writing both in complexity and diversity and suggested that Asian American writers can no longer be confined to "Asian American themes" or to "a narrow definition of Asian American identity." She concluded,

Asian American writers are better represented today than in the past, but there is a need for further efforts to encourage the production and publication of literature written about a variety of subjects from diverse Asian American perspectives that are still too little understood and appreciated by mainstream American publishers. Meanwhile, Asian American writers continue to celebrate the complexity and diversity of the Asian American experience, contributing at the same time to the ever-evolving mosaic of American literature and culture.[4]

This anthology highlights a small part of this "ever-evolving mosaic of American literature." Chinese American poetry is an integral part of Asian American literature. In their path-breaking 1974 publication, *Aiiieeeee! An Anthology of Asian American Writers*, Frank Chin, Jeffery P. Chan, Lawson F. Inada, and Shawn Wong defined Asian Americans as those "American-born and raised, who got their China and Japan from the radio, off the silver screen, from television, out of comic books, from the pushers of white American culture" and who have long been ignored and forcibly excluded from creative participation in American culture.[5] According to them, neither Asian nor American culture can define Asian American sensibility except in "the most superficial terms." In their view, there is, however, an Asian American identity and a body of Asian American literature that is neither white mimicry nor exotic artifact. Unlike writings catering to the taste of the dominant majority, this corpus of literary expressions is based on sensitive and honest depictions of Asian American experiences from Asian American viewpoints. On this basis, the four editors compiled *Aiiieeeee!* and forcefully and convincingly demonstrated that an Asian American cultural tradition exists.

While we agree with Chin et al.'s emphasis on Asian American sensibility, we consider their definition based primarily on one's nativity and ideology too restrictive. The continuing influx of Asian immigrants, including a substantial number of intellectuals, in the last three decades alone has transformed the Asian American population from a predominantly American-born population to a largely foreign-born one and has given rise to a voluminous body of literary works, mostly in Asian languages and literary forms, yet showing some of the sensitivity identified by *Aiiieeeee*'s editors. We argue, therefore, for a more inclusive definition, as suggested by Kai-yu Hsu, David Hsin-fu Wand, Elaine Kim, and Amy Ling. This anthology is a testimony to the richness and diversity of Chinese American poetry. It also demonstrates why we should be more inclusive. For example, there are novelists and poets who were born in China and who did not start to learn English until their adulthood. Stephen Liu, who is truly bilingual, is a case in point. Another gifted poet, Li-Young Lee, did not learn English until his family immigrated to America when he was about ten years old.

China, a country with about three thousand years of poetic tradition which has exerted an immense influence on the world of poetry, is bound to affect either directly or indirectly poetry writing among the overseas Chinese. Through oral and written traditions transmitted from generation to generation among the Chinese in the United States and through cultural and international exchanges in intellectual circles, Chinese Americans have been and will continue to be affected by China's strong poetic tradition. It is a constant call to poets of Chinese ancestry now dispersed in other lands and talking in diverse tongues. Though different poets will have varying attitudes towards this tradition, ranging from those such as Carolyn Lau and Arthur Sze, who embrace the tradition enthusiastically, to others such as Nellie Wong and Genny Lim, who view the tradition with ambivalent feelings, no one can ignore the tradition as though it has no relevance to his or her poetry writing.

This is a unique collection with a significant relationship to two distinctively different poetic traditions, Chinese and American. A documentation of the continuity as well as far-reaching changes in the Chinese poetic tradition and simultaneously a contribution to a much-neglected aspect of contemporary American poetry, this collection is being published separately in Chinese in China and in English in the United States. It is the first venture of its kind; we are certain it will not be the last.

Chinese American poets who write in English are mostly the descendants of pre-World War II Chinese immigrants who were predominantly peasants and merchants from China's southeastern Guangdong province. Racially segregated, economically discriminated against, and politically disenfranchised, the pre-war immigrants were forced to live as second-class "aliens ineligible to citizenship" in ghettos in major American cities called Chinatowns, which survive today not only as monuments of American institutional racism but also as traditional centers or symbols of Chinese American social, political, and cultural life. For many a Chinese American, Chinatown is the sole link they have with their ancestors and the distant land whence the latter came.

For quite a number of Chinese American authors, the Chinatown experience, or a Chinatown-type of community, is an unforgettable memory or an embodiment of Chinese American history. Nellie Wong's poem, "My Chinese Love," makes this clear:

> My Chinese love does not climb the moongate toward heaven
> nor flowers in a garden of peonies and chrysanthemums.

> My Chinese love lives in the stare of a man in a coolie hat,
> smiling to himself, content in the meanderings of his mind.

This memory is kept at the expense of "Chinese culture." For her uncle, who was a cook but suffered from an addiction to opium, the poet has stronger feelings than the remote "concubines and priestesses" in the imperial palace in Beijing. Wing Tek Lum, the Hawaiian poet, proudly calls this cultural association a "local sensibility," by which he refers to the particular environment in which poets acquired their self-consciousness as people or as poets of a particular kind.

This "Chinatown syndrome" is not necessarily geographically defined. "Local" here means a culturally localized scope of experience. In Alan Lau's poems we find not the characteristic Chinatown ambience but, rather, a powerful nostalgia for what his parents and grandparents lived and felt. In his poem, "Water That Springs from a Rock," this experience is expanded to the whole history of Chinese in America. Recalling the 1885 massacre of Chinese mine workers in Rock Springs, Wyoming, Lau's poem points directly to the feeling of those Chinese Americans who still see themselves as victims of racism in a white-dominated society here and now.

As strong and dominating as this historical symbolism is in Chinese American consciousness, it would be wrong to say that all Chinese American poets find this tradition very attractive. Some actually harbor resentment against it. In fact, to many of them, Chinatown is the personification of backwardness, bitterness, degradation, and collective humiliation, just as it represented corruption, slavery, alienness, treachery, and immorality to some whites. Many Chinese American women poets, like Chinese American novelist Jade Snow Wong, especially feel the oppressive patriarchal and sexist aspects of Chinatown life, which carries with it a message most present-day women find abhorrent, repressive, and unbearable. Such sentiment is expressed emphatically in the poems of some of the women poets in this anthology. Diane Mark, for example, warns white men, in "Suzie Wong Does Not Live Here," not to try to find their sexy Oriental dolls in Chinese American women:

> no one here
> but
> ourselves
>   stepping on,
> without downcast eyes,
> without calculating dragon power,
> without tight red cheongsams
>   embroidered with peonies
> without the
> silence

> that you've come to
> know so well
> and we,
> to feel so alien with

Other Chinese American women poets also feel acutely the need to maintain a critical distance toward the Chinese tradition, which is patriarchal and discriminatory toward women. Marilyn Chin in her poem, "So Lost in Him," which dramatizes the devotion typical of Asian women, ironically fills her poem with beautiful "Oriental images" that normally accompany a traditional love poem:

> In the morning, half way down
> toward the tended grove,
> bamboo and acacia tangled.
> So lost in him, she couldn't feel
> the underbrush, wet with dew,
> soaking her zori and
> the hem of her new dungarees,
> nor the fawn dying within her.

And though Shirley Lim, a poet born in a Malaysian Chinese family, feels sad in front of her father's grave for failing to be a filial child, she finds that she has no other choice except to live an entirely different life.

> He did not live for my returning.
> News came after burial.
> I did not put on straw, black,
> Gunny-sack, have not fastened
> Grief on shoulder, walked mourning
> Behind, pouring grief before him,
> Not submitted to his heart.
>
> This then must be enough, . . .
> For nights, remembering bamboo
> And bats cleared in his laughter.
> My father's daughter, I pour
> No brandy before memory,
>
> But labour, constantly labour,
> Bearing sunwards grave bitter smoke.

In Carolyn Lau's works, the rebellion against Chinese tradition takes a breathtaking twist toward an attempt to demolish the Electra complex. In "On the Fifth Anniversary of My Father's Death," the poet confesses her sexual attraction toward her father but ends the poem with a surprising macabre warning:

> If it is true that after a person dies
> the spirit can hear and see its past life
> I want you to know, Daddy,
> I'm glad you're dead.

The semi-deified father figure, so essential to traditional Chinese mentality, is then devastatingly humanized and, with it, oppressive male dominance.

The de-traditionalized image in which some poets are proudly depicting themselves is totally modern, seemingly without any national legacy. Marilyn Chin sneers in her poem, "So Lost in Him," at the role women are supposed to play: in her view, it is ridiculously slavish. In another poem, "A Chinaman's Chance," she provides a devastating negation of a Chinatown tradition full of pain and agony, too broken and weak to ensure the survival of Chinese Americans.

> The railroad killed your great-grandfather
> His arms here, his legs there . . .
> *How can we remake ourselves in his image?*
>
> Your father worked his knuckles black
> So you might have pink cheeks. Your father
> Burped you on the back; why must you water his face?

This is the cultural dilemma most Chinese Americans find painful yet difficult to escape, a dilemma, they feel, that was created and defined by the dominant society. In their effort to seek roots, Chinese Americans found their roots easy to uncover: they had always been there. Perhaps this is the reason that such roots are not attractive: they still live and thus cannot be romanticized. Wing Tek Lum, who once condemned assimilation into American society as "becoming a mule," that is, "perforce sterile," finds the steak on his table of a very peculiar nature in "T-Bone Steak":

> No, it was not
> Chinese, much less
> American, that pink piece
> sitting in my rice
> bowl.

As many Chinese American poets see it, such a situation places them on the periphery of American society and turns them into what sociologists call marginal men. They suffer from a lack of attachment,

ment, but they also gain the advantage of being able to choose commitment to either culture. They have the frustration of lacking connections to society, but they can more easily adopt a critical distance vis-à-vis that society.

Social criticism or protest, then, sounds a dissonant note in the works of Chinese American poets. This characteristic shows up in works of the former San Francisco group, Unbound Feet Six, which broke up on ideological differences in the late 1970s. Three of its members, Nellie Wong, Merle Woo, and Genny Lim, whose works appear in this anthology, still keep their critical spirit—a spirit manifested in the sympathy toward the downtrodden and the miserable. As Merle Woo puts it,

> Yellow woman, a revolutionary speaks:
>
> "They have mutilated our genitals, but I will
>   restore them;
> I will render our shames and praise them,
> Our beauties, our mothers:
> Those young Chinese whores on display in barracoons;
> the domestics in soiled aprons;
> the miners, loggers, railroad workers
>   holed up in Truckee in winters.
>   I will create armies of their descendants. . . ."

The same critical stance appears in Arthur Sze's "Listening to a Broken Radio" and Shalin Hai-Jew's "Kinged." It also can be seen in a more ambivalent way in the subtle and ironical criticism of the American dream of success in such poems as John Yau's "Rumors":

> An architect wants to build a house
> rivaling the mountains surrounding
> his sleep, each turret mute as a hat.
> He crosses a river to reach ground
> hard enough to begin his plan. He crosses
> a river the way a river crosses his sleep,
> swirling with questions.

Arthur Sze's poem, "The Aphrodisiac," is another good example of implicit criticism of the American way of life, where aggressiveness and ambition are highly praised but look out of place when they come into contact with another culture:

> "Power is my aphrodisiac."
> Power enables him to
> connect a candle-lit dinner
> to the landing on the moon.

He sees a plot in the acid
content of American soil,
malice in a configuration
of palm leaf shadows.
He is obsessed with
the appearance of democracy
in a terrorized nation.

Criticism of that which is taken as natural in American culture can
likewise be observed in such poems as Marilyn Chin's "A Dream in the
Life of an American Joe" and Wing Tek Lum's "A Moment of the Truest
Terror," which focus on the role the United States plays in the Third
World.

Being critical of America does not mean that Chinese American
poets are blind to the shortcomings in Chinese culture. Being outside of
China provides some of them with a sharper insight into the
deficiencies of that culture. Stephen Liu, who remains more connected
to China than the others in this anthology, depicts this in a dramatic
way in "My Father's Martial Art":

From a busy street I brood over high cliffs
on O Mei, where my father and his Master sit:
shadows spread across their faces as the smog
between us deepens into a funeral pyre.

But don't retreat into night, my father.
Come down from the cliffs. Come
with a single Black Dragon Sweep and hush
this oncoming traffic with your *hah, hah, hah.*

The impotence of Chinese martial art confronting the modern world
brings the poem to a frustrating, comic ending.

Artistically, the works of Chinese American poets cover a much
wider range than can be imagined from the term "Chinese American."
The stylistic adaptability of Chinese American poets convinces us that
a monolithic artistic perspective would surely fall short of presenting
Chinese American poetry in all its colors.

John Yau, a New York-based art critic by profession, is a poet who
has a close association with the New York School of contemporary
poetry which has a strong inclination toward surrealism. The
experience of Manhattan brings itself into a language distorted under
the intensity of urban pressure. Some of his poems read like a Dali
painting: they are phantasmagoria full of cruel images of modern life.
Thus in "Third Variation on Corpse and Mirror,"

two dogs played catch
with someone's head,
while a hand waved good-bye
to the body it once carried.

This horror does not live only in an imagination squeezed by the intensity of experience; it lives, too, in daily life. The late night movies, the coffin factories in Massachusetts or in a neighbor's garden, all undergo a horrified metamorphosis, as in "Carp and Goldfish":

Some fish we peel back, leaving only bones. Others devour us, leaving only the stories.

Thus, Yau's poems participate in an all-permeating fantasy. Or we might say that poetry is now more substantial than real life. John Yau is fond of teasing his readers with his playful handling of language because he seems to believe that the only way to survive is to outplay the horror of life with the uncanniness of poetry.

Diana Chang, another New York poet, is also a painter. In her poems she chases the same concise minimalism as in modern painting, trying to leave enough space in which a free artistic imagination can roam by undoing language. The rhythm of space and plane is reflected in the rhythm of language, as in "Codes":

An undulation
on too many legs
crossing the path
in such a manner as to suggest
it would blush if it were noticed

Is a cat.

Jettisoning normal balance, the syncopated rhythm in Chang's sentence structure makes the lines meaningful not only semantically but also as language itself, that is, in its very linguistic form. This self-reflection of poetic message upon itself is more visible in another poem of hers, "Implosion":

Someone says something lovely
in the late afternoon
We listen
transoms let down everywhere
meanings telling us what they mean
another sentence arrives

It seems that, to her, language can go on by itself without referents, just as in paintings, where colors and figures can be significant in their own dynamics without depicting any objects. This ideal state is not as easy to achieve in poetry as in painting. Yet Diana Chang proves that it is still a possibility worth striving for.

Mei-mei Berssenbrugge of New Mexico, in her pursuit of artistic perfection, turns her subtle experience into deftly drawn sketches with short but graceful continuous strokes, as in "The Intention of Two Rivers":

> Friday, you'll be here. Confluence
> across the delta again. A pattern fans out
> on the sand. When at lowest tide it is sunset
> I can wade across, holding my shoes.

In *Empathy*, a later collection, however, she turns to a different style, with longer lines and sentences. Her newer poems sound more like incantations. She is also a choreographer, and some of these poems, according to her, were written "as spoken texts to accompany the choreography" of her collaborators in a New York dance company.

> For me, the insignificant or everyday gesture constructs a
> choreography of parts
> and what touches me is where the inarticulate, the error or
> tension finds concrete manifestation
> and is recognized.

Here, what is important is not what the poetic discourse is about but the poetic language itself. These sentences are argumentative, but the effect of the lines comes not from argument but from the spell the swirling rhythm casts on the listeners and readers.

Alan C. Lau, a poet from the Pacific Northwest, strives to maintain a calmness in his rumination of memories and impressions of the present. In his major work, "Water that Springs from a Rock," he uses the "collage" technique seen in such major American works as William Carlos Williams' "Patterson," or black poet Robert Haydon's "The Middle Passage." Two entirely opposite styles—lyrical and historio-graphical—are juxtaposed to achieve the magnitude and emotional power of epics. The shock produced by the massacre it tells about thus becomes a solid sediment. The passion in the lyrics, which is short-lived, is thus contextualized in history and presses on present-day life.

Jason Hwang, a musician by profession, has a fine sense of control of speed in his lovely short poems, just like the contrast of successive movements in music. We can see the simple image in poems like "Uncountable" gradually building up its momentum:

> On the sand
> holding each other

> our sleep forms a
> boneless imprint
> in the sea
> wrapping ourselves, barely visible
> under a sheet of eloquent alterations,
> gestures flocking to our rippling outline
> which will not erode . . .

The context adds the pressure on the image little by little, till finally the image is developed into a conceit, a beautifully evolving symbol.

As we have already noted, almost none of the Chinese American poets can afford to ignore the Chinese poetic tradition. John Yau writes about the possibility of riveting a dream on the Chinese image; Mei-mei Berssenbrugge tries to explore the poetic space that is typically Chinese; but the poets who emphasize the Chinese poetic tradition the most are Arthur Sze and Carolyn Lau.

Arthur Sze, once a student of Chinese literature at the University of California at Berkeley, is very attentive to Chinese classical poetry. Himself a translator, he is familiar with the Chinese poets who explored the mystical art of poetry for dozens of centuries. Most of his poems, with sentences terse and compact and cut into shorter lines, avoid the argumentative rhetoric so typical of Western poetry. His short poem, "The Owl," is reminiscent of Chinese poetry not only in its form but also in the manner it creates an ambience so as to let the readers feel the poetic world mystically hidden between what is said and what is not said.

> The path was purple in the dusk.
> I saw an owl, perched,
> on a branch.
>
> And when the owl stirred, a fine dust
> fell from its wings. I was
> silent then. And felt
>
> the owl quaver. And at dawn, waking,
> the path was green in the
> May light.

It is not necessary to cite a poem from, say, Wang Wei, whom Arthur Sze admires and translates, or other Chinese masters, to prove that they share a poetic attitude. What is interesting is how this Chinese poetics is adapted to modern poetry in English. A special effect is brought about with the arrangement of the ending of the poem:

the abruptness leaves sufficient room for the readers to visualize what the poet feels so strongly—something that cannot be expressed in words.

The stylistic and thematic diversity of Chinese American poetry defeats any stereotyping of ethnocentricity. Even in Idaho, the Chinese American poetic voice is not silent. In his poems, Alex Kuo sings more about the rugged landscape of the Pacific Northwest than about any other thing. He finds comfort in the overpowering austerity of nature—a Chinese American poet who feels that only the purifying loneliness of mountains and waters can be a true source of poetic inspiration. The seemingly impersonal, stand-offish lines in his poems contain fervent poetic feelings that chase incessantly the true meaning of life.

As if to serve as a contrast, Li-Young Lee, a Chicago interior designer, enthralls us with his gently emotional poems. With a lyrical gift rarely seen in modern poetry, he turns what seems to be commonplaces in life, in personal relations, into songs that express the eternal joy or sorrow of love, of death, of recollection, and of forgetting, a quality that, according to Gerald Stern, boils down to "a pursuit of certain Chinese ideas, or Chinese memories," as can be seen in "My Indigo":

> Little sister, my indigo,
> my secret, vaginal and sweet,
> you unfurl yourself shamelessly
> toward the ground. You burn. You live
> a while in two worlds
> at once.

A disarming charm, natural, easy-going, yet extremely sincere, makes it a sheer delight to read Lee's poems. The publication of his first collection, *Rose*, marks the beginning of a productive career for a highly promising Chinese American poet.

In contrast to Arthur Sze and Li-Young Lee, Carolyn Lau seems more interested in Chinese philosophy. According to her, she became an active poet only after she took up serious study of Chinese philosophy, which, somehow, got mixed with the folktales, fairy tales, and ghost stories many Chinese Americans hear in their childhood. The language Carolyn Lau uses is not an easy one to understand. There are lots of allusions, some historical, some personal. Often there is no obvious continuity of rhetoric or sequencing of events. One has to be attentive to discover what the poet is thinking but not saying, as in "A Footnote to a Dispute among Confucius's Disciples":

> Wife or not, I turn to look
> at what was Right before my breath.

> The white horse yields a world
> of words defying music's eyes.
>
> I cannot, can
> not stop desire's choice to pleasure in my worth.
> The birds instruct me in the art
> to follow senses known at birth.

To fathom this poem, readers must know a little about the dispute between the Mencius school and the Xunzi school in China on whether man is good or evil at birth. This dispute ended with the former winning, thus establishing Confucianism more as an ethical and political system than as a religion in China. Carolyn Lau does not appear to join in the dispute; what she insists on is the right of human beings to choose pleasure and to "follow senses known at birth," the best of which is poetry, or poetic instinct in everyman: "words defying music's eyes." Thus she turns the table in her dispute with traditionalists by using their own weapons.

Some other poems of hers are easier to read and follow, but a little knowledge of Chinese philosophy is still required to understand them. This short poem seems to be a little sentimental about daily life if we miss the clue dropped in the title:

> I spread from the bottom of mountain
> inside tree. Giving the valley
> echo. Everyday, the river of
> steady sail, permitting
> desire. All my body grows flower
> as feed for children, as if
> I am a most important thing on earth.

The title is "One Meaning of Dao." Zhuangzi, the Daoist (Taoist) philosopher, once discussed where the great Dao (Tao), the supreme truth, could be found. He insisted that Dao "goes gradually down," till it reaches the commonest thing in the world. Thus Dao can be with every humble human being engaged in the most vulgar activities of daily life. What we must know is only how to find it. Carolyn Lau finds Dao in herself and in whatever her eyes fall upon. What is more, she believes Dao can be passed on to one's children as a precious spiritual heritage, as flowers out of one's body.

Different Chinese American poets, emerging with confidence and optimism, are going in very different directions, making Chinese American poetry a prism with many facets, a long spectrum with many colors. They have created something uniquely American, rooted, however, in a sensitivity uniquely Chinese American. Any monolithic reading of Chinese American poetry will be counterproductive. Still we can discern some trends in the movement—to quote Mei-mei Berssenbrugge, "the fanning out of the river."

On the one hand, Chinese American poets have been striving to reach a new, more balanced, and appreciative stance toward the heritage of Chinatown and of China, while on the other hand, they are also taking critical stands toward Chinese or Chinese American tradition. Ancestor worship, in the eyes of the poets, is no help in this world.

In poems by such militant poets as Marilyn Chin and Nellie Wong, the perspective reaches beyond ethnic sensibility. A common cause for justice and equality transcends the boundary of skin color. Merle Woo's poem, "A Liŋuistik", tries to convince us that the spirit is not bound by nationality or a particular language. When Carolyn Lau meets Guanyin, the female Bodhisattva, the reaffirmation is given in feminist terms—a stance enthusiastically endorsed by today's Chinese American women.

Jason Hwang, for his part, in "Myself" imagines his reunion with his father in "the arriving presence" which is also "a miraculous wash of prehistory."

> I stand close to where my father has stood
> footprints brushed on to the beach with dark blue ink
> a lyric notation
> of a joyous reunion.

The happiness of a solution? For most Chinese American poets it is premature to seek one. The necessity of embracing, but at the same time distancing themselves from, their cultural roots gives their works a unique tension.

The last question that needs to be asked is what position Chinese American poetry occupies in contemporary American poetry. Some scholars hold that minority culture can maintain its independence only by keeping itself outside the mainstream, so as not to lose its particularities. Can Chinese American poets find a way to get into the mainstream while retaining particularities of their own?

Often overlooked is the fact that modern American poetry has been under constant Chinese influence ever since the days of the so-called American Poetry Renaissance. Consider Ezra Pound, Amy Lowell, Witter Bynner, Conrad Aiken, Kenneth Rexroth, William Carlos Williams, and others. Chinese classical poetry and philosophy have also been associated with some important names in modern American poetry. When contemporary American poetry rose with an anti-academic cry in the late 1950s, Chinese poetry and philosophy were among its mainsprings. Gary Snyder became a hero of the counter-culture because he tried to incorporate the Zen-Dao idea of maintaining harmony between self and nature; Robert Bly wanted to find a way to strike a balance between the Yin of poetic spirit and the Yang of poetic form; James Wright reached back to Chinese poets to discover the horror of pollution in post-industrial Minneapolis; Allen Ginsberg looked for new insights in his recent impressions of China; Charles Wright endeavored to incorporate Chinese philosophy in the surrealistic imagination; Carolyn Kizer tried to turn the dynamics of the Chinese worldview into a confrontation between Yin and Yang poetics; Jackson MacLow strived to discover a transcending force in Chinese philosophy over the pressure of rationalist language. There is a much longer list: Kenneth O. Hanson, Lucien Stryk, Frederick Morgan, Robert Barnstone . . .

Facing this "mainstream" phenomenon, Chinese American poets find themselves in a peculiar position. Since Chinese American poetry is part of contemporary American poetry, with a special "inherited" relationship to China, Chinese American poets could, and should form a link (an intermedium, to borrow a term from comparative literature), or, if they are more successful, a vanguard in this trend.

This is, in fact, how some Chinese American poets have been entering the mainstream of American poetry. Chinese American poetry is finally moving beyond the "ethnic magazines." Some collections by Chinese American poets have already appeared in the publication list of "big presses," though such appearance is by no means a proper measure of the achievement of Chinese American poetry, especially when it is still trying to find its own voice. However, many of the poets included here already feel that something new is taking place in Chinese American poetry. As Marilyn Chin reminds us in "The End of a Beginning," the new is not easy to come by:

> . . . and I,
> the beginning of an end, the end of a beginning,
> sit here, drink unfermented green tea . . .
> . . . I have
> the answers to your last riddles

L. Ling-chi Wang
Henry Yiheng Zhao

Notes

[1]Most of her works appeared in the California magazine, *Land of Sunshine.*

[2]*A Pagoda of Jewels* (New York: Joseph A. Elison, 1920).

[3]Exceptions are two novels by H. T. Tsiang, a Chinese bohemian who lived in New York's Greenwich Village, which describe the life of Chinese outcasts in the United States in the years of the Great Depression. Disappointed with his literary career, he became a Hollywood actor in 1940. His works are finally starting to attract the attention of literary historians.

[4]Elaine H. Kim, "Asian American Writers: A Bibliographical Review," *American Studies International* XXII:2 (1984), p. 69.

[5]Frank Chin, et al., *Aiiieeeee!: An Anthology of Asian-American Writers* (New York: Anchor books, 1975), pp. ix-x.

MEI-MEI BERSSENBRUGGE

Born to a Chinese mother and a Dutch-American father, Mei-mei Berssenbrugge received her B.A. from Reed College, Oregon, and her M.F.A. degree from Columbia. Her poems have appeared in many magazines and anthologies. She is the author of several collections of poetry: *Summits Move with the Tide* (1974), *Random Possession* (1979), *The Heat Bird* (1984), and *Empathy* (1987). She has collaborated and performed with the choreographer Theodora Yoshikami in New York City. Her own play, *One, Two Cups* was staged in New York and Seattle. She has taught in universities in Alaska, Ohio, New Mexico, and Colorado, and is an editor of *Conjunctions* magazine.

If I try to think about my poetics, I think of the material sensation of placing one word next to another word. The words feel to me like objects with weight and density. The operation of combining two words feels to me like an operation in physics, which releases great energy.

If I try to think about my poetic tradition, I think about Tu Fu and Li Po and Wang Wei. But also Sappho, Dante, Yeats, Vallejo, Rilke, Stein, Whitman, Dickinson, Pound, Ashbery.

It has been important for me to try and articulate an aesthetic of what I can know, and to place this aesthetic in an emotional and humane context.

It has been important for me to explore elements of form in language, as a means of exploring this aesthetic.

The Intention of Two Rivers

1

I remember the spring flowers
how frail white petals appeared that were wax
with roots deeper than we could dig
Everywhere along the riverbank, with the river flowing
we found unknown ones that bloom only during a wet spring
promises that are rare and tough, but periodically remade
They made us happy. We took turns holding back willows

When the river is an alkaline trickle again
along its old outsize track, we are both gone
I imagine the different pods, leather and intricate
as hardballs, cracked by animals, carried, rolled
around, asleep, and full of seed

2

It is the direction of a river changes
with separation. The reference point now
is the sea, a dam, fixed like salt on a leaf
but the current is still strong. Only, it points
dories upstream of ropes. Rivercrabs still move
freely on the floor and gently prod each other

Friday, you'll be here. Confluence
across the delta again. A pattern fans out
on the sand. When at lowest tide it is sunset
I can wade across, holding my shoes

Mei-mei Berssenbrugge

Suspension Bridge

You say all of us
even if we fail become lights
along the awesome bones. Separated
by darkness, humming through wires
on windy nights, bellying out
you're so sure the current is personal

Not like the firefly
that lives for a month
jolted at random by a blank force
that never knows the brightness
of its shocked body
even on cool nights above the grasses
when it loves, victim to victim

Mei-mei Berssenbrugge

The proportions of a body to blue eyes
big as locusts are made frictionless by distance
After the war, the design of refrigerators
became classical in proportion. He told her
the Chinese put halves of a settee on opposite
sides of a room, but she preferred a white jar's
closing arc to the sky, like the arms of two hills
holding it. He disdained her fear. He stopped saving
wishbones for her, or knotholes depicting the galaxies
She understood he was making himself the gap

Mei-mei Berssenbrugge

This is a section of the poem "Pack Rat Sieve."

The Eurasian at the party would not speak to her. Little lights
inside paper sacks cast willow flames on the snow
the little lights that line paths
of the courtyard. You have to assume each is the same, so
the maze recedes and is not a vertical map of varying sacks
on a blank wall, since it is dark, oh
Mei-mei, you've walked in that garden before. I'm sick of
these dry gardens. Everyone tells me I should get angry at him
The nun's voice quavered behind a screen. There was a shadow
voice to hers of another one singing quietly and
a little off. I prefer to think it was the light back
How can he dream of tying me to his bed, in a blizzard
with snow to my thigh? He tells me I am flirting
with the void. I am not Chinese. I invite him to step
out to the garden for plum blossoms. They would be
very beautiful, now. Their petals would
blanket the snow like snow on sand
but it is morning

Mei-mei Berssenbrugge

This is a section of the poem "Pack Rat Sieve."

On the Mountain with the Deer

When the deer grazing upwind
from where we lay on the mountain suddenly
heard my voice, whirled and crashed
against an oak, we began to run, too

Then I knew animals burst into flame
on meeting each other in the woods
I overlooked spring shoots. Only pine
trees shaded a patch of thawed ground
a rabbit in winter fur, and a lynx

Even meeting your own, eyes widen
and the throat swallows back escape
I'm not saying your hand feels like a lizard
when you think you are comforting me

There are always poisonous lizards on my back
the prey of our hands touching the dark

Mei-mei Berssenbrugge

Duration of Water

So that I make you a microcosm or symbolic center of the public
like a theatre, with hundreds of painted scenes combining and recombining
in order to exaggerate situations of joy or pain on stage, instead of
five short songs about you, accompanying dancers who seem to float on
    their backs
in still water, as the empyrean. They would be the water motor. Three
    stones
protrude from the water and three instruments combine and repeat a
    simple scale,
but some passions only resolve with fire and weather catastrophes.
The orchestra nevertheless clears like foliage
for Yang Kuei Fei's sigh, when she hears the emperor wants her.
There is a red line on the boards I can follow in the thick smoke
or mist. The shoulders of the man change scale, as if I had
been manipulating the field inside a small box, to see how light
can transform me into foliage, as a sexual punishment. The music
can take on the cold or heat of the air like blue chameleons on the limbs
    of the tree,
as if you could look through the leaves into the empyrean. I can turn back
my sleeve with the multiplicity of detail of the battleground. The colors
combine into legible hues at a distance. There is a craft at work
to reconcile emotion in a purely speculative ambience,
tracking the last aria, like a duration of water
which is a piece of white silk.

Mei-mei Berssenbrugge

8

The Margin

A sense of being responsible for a crisis may also give a feeling of
    control. Victims
prefer to accept blame and guilt that entails to admitting that life is
    unfair,
a curtain of air as its margin of yielding for the sake of her emotion.
    The way a peach-colored
amaryllis can cut up the space of a room, depending on how he places it
    in the room, an environment erodes.
An invisible plane of air is almost undetectable to touch as you walked
    down into the canyon,
laden with hue. It moves horizontally along the crestline, but varies
    vertically in temperature,
making a complex profile in cold shade from where I look onto
    illuminated planes of the far cliff's face.

The air seems very complicated to sense or very subtle, because it is very
    difficult to relate
to a particular pleasure or pain. This is because so much imagination is
    involved.
Instead of the situation of rock climbing or making love, bringing a
    person into the present,
unobstructed space is very provocative, because it is ubiquitous. It seeks to
    express
a wall, rather than be contained within or dependent on the wall as a
    separated object,
or as striations around a branching weed, or the memory of snowing for
    half an hour in it.

A crestline is red, but the lower wall and I are in blue shadow,
because of the implication of gravity holding air around the amaryllis
    and versus
the weightlessness of light on selected cliff faces complexly structured
    into lines and cords
as an experience of one version of the body. A belief in personal
    invulnerability to caprice
disintegrates slowly with the pulls and weights of the body in motion,
whereas unobstructed space is very, very plain.

Although no site is transferrable, images of a site become more and more
    abstract through color.
They also charge with fiction when revealed as shot from the point of
    view of a couple

in a helicopter, a surveillance of peach-colored snow on volcanic ash,
    seeming static figures.
Then the strip surprises you by changing or seeming to change ever so
    slightly
in the shadow of the mountain. You see a broad luminous horizon of desert
in the distance, an allusive expanse of expanded, indifferent purity.
Because your eye clings to this margin, it appears to speed up.

Mei-mei Berssenbrugge

The Star Field

Placing our emotion on a field, I said, became a nucleus of space,
defined by a rain of light and indeterminate contours of a landscape
like the photograph of an explosion, and gave the travel of your gaze into
    it, or on me,
imaginative weight of the passage along a gulf of space
or a series of aluminum poles.

She walks through rooms of blue chain-linked fence, a spacious tennis court
of rooms on concrete, instead of the single movement of a room, where
    sky and earth
would come together.

Outside is the field she is thinking about: a category of gray dots
on a television screen of star data, representing no one's experience,
but which thrills all who gaze on it, so it must be experience, and
the land at large becomes the light on the land.

A coyote or a flicker's call
is transfixed at the moment before its dissemination across the field,
a sediment of, instead
of the trace of feeling, the ratio of people to the space.

I pass through blue focal planes as a scene of desire.
The material of the sky adjacent to me eludes me, a pure signifier,
shifting sense, the sky or space a gradation of material, the light
a trace of mobility like a trace of light on a sensitive screen,
extended into the plane of the trace
and marked by light poles or drawn close by a planet at the edge.

Your name becomes a trace of light. Through
its repetition and deferral, my life protects itself
from blurs, time lapses, flares
of the sexual act, its mobility of an afterimage.

Then I can understand the eye's passage into depth
as an inability to stand still for you to see.

Mei-mei Berssenbrugge

Naturalism

1

He calls it instincts and their vicissitudes, or emotions, at the border
in blue and white. The river ice moves down the open channel of the river
or it moves up the river. It is a dishevelled stripe of ice moving past
ice piled on the bank, like a filmstrip along the lens of ice, and
it seems most personal when the tide changes, across forty-five minutes,
    almost indiscernibly,
so that the mode of my feeling was taken care of simply by the demands
    of observing it.
The overcast goes into patches of blue and the clouds whiten,
as if television cameras were suspended above and reflected in the water,
which takes on a sheen of aluminum in bright sun.

2

A feeling moves like a hand across the blue and white mountain range
   in bright sun, after
a plain of little white clouds breaks up. The agitation of personal
   experience
was thought to becloud its intellectual content,
when the mode of an act could be taken care of simple by the demands of
   the feeling-at-hand,
its effort to unify the meaning of discontinuous affections,
formally allusive to plains for unity. My feeling was not mystical but
   conjectural.
Its naturalism is an authentic source of pathos, delicate and precise,
but it is not good manners to him.

3

A live bird joins the flock of birds across the bay, the flock
in soft focus behind the windowpanes, of snow, stars or flowers.
How an emotion grew out of or failed to grow out of the landscape
was the most important determinant of the ties it later formed with him,
an attempt to wrest from landscape itself what others got from relations,
its performance of innate or unconscious dexterity. Wind became a symbol
for resistance of the thing being depicted to its depiction, or
    conventionalization
into the pathos of good manners.

4

I have to communicate to you the possibilities of fantasy, the possibility
     that the real world
could be different from the apparent. But I have no confidence. Only
an erotic concentration on a vicissitude of light,
so the visual part is my mirage
for my memory of the landscape. The image of reality and mirage are
     mixed, so you see *through,*
under the control of the camera with my arm and my emotion.

5

The while is long with the speed of time. It is a camera controlled by
    the participant,
so the speed and the time control the image, too. The feeling is the
    afterimage of yourself
you are always coming to, so I like landscape where coming to the feeling
is always elemental or hierarchical. Or
if camera sounds too harsh or formal for this elusive process, we can just
    say, we
grasp an imaginative continuity that corresponds to the landscape,
creating an emotion greater than what can be accounted for
by its blue and white plains.

6

What can be at stake with an emotion is not a location and its occupation,
but the capacity to move more or less at will. The coast's use of feedback
    can steady
and bring into unison several stages of the emotion with great elegance.
My own experiences of it ranged from the therapeutic to a more
    constrained, task-oriented
intuition. This is a direct effect of my empathic involvement,
a persistent, attentive involvement with you,
although it is impossible to control the body as the object.
You can remember how the far grass on a sandbar lit up, as at the end of
    an afternoon lightning storm
on a foreground range of waves. When
I walked before the waves, they were pieced by a row of lights at a low
    level, like footlights.

7

I had continued to a state of exhaustion when a control channel broke down,
but the exhaustion is reversible,
as when a video camera is a quartz stone on a plane of mica
in sunlight so bright it becomes silence.
There is no outside communication, and you think I have gone over the
        edge. I had
a sort of nostalgia about it. In the same sense that the emotion was too
        vehement in the beginning,
I had this nostalgia, this deep regret at having to return to normal, but
I could do nothing to prolong or shorten it.

Mei-mei Berssenbrugge

DIANA CHANG

Diana Chang was born of a Chinese father and an Eurasian mother in New York. Her first collection of poems, *The Horizon Is Definitely Speaking*, was published in 1982, followed by *What Matisse Is After* in 1984. She is the author of six published novels, *The Frontiers of Love, A Woman of Thirty, A Passion for Life, The Only Game in Town, Eye to Eye*, and *A Perfect Love*. Before beginning to write novels, she was an editor in various publishing houses. As a painter, she has had solo shows and has also appeared in group exhibitions. She is Adjunct Associate Professor of English at Barnard College where she teaches creative writing.

I have said elsewhere that I feel I'm an American writer whose background is mostly Chinese.

My novels and short stories seem to be preoccupied with being and identity, and arise out of my abiding passion for exploring character and emotion to create the psychological realities of particular situations.

In some of my poems a self speaks to the self. Or I write of poetry itself or I explore the natural world and its soul, as it were. In style, I hope to be imagistic, moving instinctively among metaphor, simile, and personification, in order to make my ideas concrete and tangible.

A Wall of Their Own

Weeping, a woman is watching
    her friend's back in a mirror
        say nothing at all

"Get lost," a man says.
    His child smiles still harder,
        closing another door

Near windows, birds seeking more flight,
    crash into sky,
        struck dead by images

Dreaming they are well, the dying
    through walls lifting like wings
        slip away

A lady espaliered
    on love
        loves walls

Diana Chang

Keeping Time

Tell me:
It is not happening this summer
when the word "when"

can be a habitation
baffling animals which run through

The out-of-doors tries to bank itself in rooms,
the roof a skin translucent with nothingness

Another death in our neighborhood—
life's been put aside again

In order to not move on:
paintings must recede
into the painter

who hopes to be glad
to be less realized

Tell me this summer
nothing is happening here

Insist on it

Diana Chang

Things Are for Good

The ocean is practicing white writing on its liquid tablet
never done finding out what it needs to say
Day after day the afternoon develops itself in arias
    lofted across the earth

Each summer walls of wheat recur,
trees change and prevail

On any side of the world
beyond friends and ties

what happens
happens

miraculously now
and again now

The moon, too, has no visible means of support
It wills its way across the night

Diana Chang

Codes

An undulation
on too many legs
crossing the path
in such a manner as to suggest
it would blush if it were noticed

Is a cat.

These people
who have still to stop smiling and be introduced
might move you to cry out

If you knew their names.

A lack of words feels like dusk:
We are not blind but we are uncertain we see.

Its pain is matched
by this other remorse for names

Which bring them to mind truly,
falsely—

mountains
women
fish

Diana Chang

Implosion

Someone says something lovely
in the late afternoon

We listen

transoms let down everywhere
meanings telling us what they mean
another sentence arrives

girls ponder men as always

He moves over
The sofa understands much more after that

a scene has begun
The novel writes itself on the ceiling
    of everyone's head:

I said, she said I said
He declares we heard us laugh

before you know it you've been written up

and titled

It's an ordinary story that murmured
in the ordinary way reflections reflect

on us flying apart
as characters come to lie

in our beds

Diana Chang

The Kiss

I sprouted in a rain of people.

Birds budded unseen between us
    rushed into me.

I was deafened by their taffeta.

I looked into your eyes to see
but surprise is only green.

Suddenly, I teetered
as though you are tall,
a friend flown in a crowd,
a friend newfound.

We drew far away.
We went near.

Diana Chang

What Matisse Is After

The straight in a curve
is what Matisse is after

two lines
one veering in,

an invitation to
the rest of space,
the other

a long gourd
swelling
out of bone

an arm sings
that its reach

rounds
into a heave
of loving

the line of a thigh
on its departure
toward returning

in the teeth
of our dying

what elegant
flying

He exhales paint we need

to
breathe

Diana Chang

Present Tense

Before her in the mirror she sees
the Persian hanging which is behind her

and three apparitions of the ocean
36" x 36" or 14" x 16"

No tide splashes the radio beneath
where a shadow is snagged on stillness

White sofa, black chairs, Victorian bureau, covered dish
magically make themselves scarce whenever she is
    somewhere else
and even when she's lost only in thought

As if someone whispered
she's had no history before this room,
they bring her to attention now

To think that from the beginning she's had no way
with things
Her imagination wouldn't have been so poor either
to take, without struggling, this and these

She swears she would have hailed a galleon riding
or arabesqued across Adriatic terraces, nothing measured in
    inches

Her years work out their news
the way its web
is the spider's unhurried career
toward how she is here

incapable of wishing
for the moon
which, 2" x 4",

harnesses
blood
and
sea

Diana Chang

Swimmers

They rose to the surface together
to find the membrane of the water was the sky—
too empty, too blinding

Struggling to remain unawake,
each pitched the other into sensation

Four arms, thighs made one anemone
undulating toward shade in which to see,
to know that in such coming tides everything could live

Tethered by undertow, they poured for each other.
This keelhauling her true element . . .
became his wasting flood, his brink of drowning

Empty, too, extinguished utterly, he sought in the sky
a dry sounding called aloneness
transcending as ice, as fire

Shedding the deep, he climbed into day
and without a seafarer's turning
was gone

Blue was stained into her, not his eyes

The great lake still shakes with memory:
unsteadied, altered as had pleased them

Motion—squalling, purling—moves and yet stays.
He went first. For ages, tears swam after him.

Now she too is part of the shore

Diana Chang

A Persuasion

Music at large rends the air
  while I complain.
Against my grain,
  music proclaims.
I talk.

It cries against dying.
Mountains are brought to light.
Skies spread about.

Hand over hand
  music climbs.
All it realizes
  it consumes.

Each freighted phrase
  withheld
  then placed

  note by note
  in my heart

I deplore this hurtful
  attention.

It presses
  for my promise
  to shun all the rest.
I fret instead.

Shy of grace, I am borne
  across its ranging breadth.

I ask: Why
  does this gift
  so contest a life
  I am used to bearing?

Riven,
my blood is ether,
and I beg mercy
of such art.

Plagued, my breath
        joins the driving rack.
Fields sweep me out,
        leeways lie
        steeped in snow.

Woodwinds slake me with ice.

Shivering, I speak
        against their awesome
        adjurations

And lose, as always,
        the argument.
Blue and meek,
        chattering,
I begin to sing . . . .

Diana Chang

MARILYN CHIN

Marilyn Chin is the author of *Dwarf Bamboo* (Greenfield Review Press, 1987) and is currently on the faculty of the M.F.A. program at San Diego State University. Her poetry has appeared recently in the *Iowa Review, Ploughshares* and *Parnassus* and is included in the Norton *Introduction to Poetry*. She is the recipient of a Stegner Fellowship, a National Endowment for the Arts Writing Fellowship, and a Mary Robert Rinehart Award. In the late 1970s she was a translator for the International Writing Program at the University of Iowa, where she worked as translator for the poet Ai Qing (*The Selected Poems of Ai Qing*, Indiana University Press). She majored in ancient Chinese literature at the University of Massachusetts at Amherst and received her MFA in poetry from Iowa in 1981. She was born in Hong Kong, grew up in Portland, Oregon and the San Francisco Bay Area, and has taught as well at UCLA.

A poet, certainly, has her work cut out for her. She may spend days contemplating on the next sentence, or on the next image, or on something as abstract or ambitious as an idea. For the Chinese American poet, she may dwell on the problems of her bi-cultural identity, on assimilation, on political and global questions . . . etc. . . . .

However, I believe that the most formidable challenge is that presented by the art itself. Yeats once called out to his fellow countrymen, "Irish poets, learn your trade." My eternal struggle as a poet is to perfect my craft, to strive for excellence, to "learn my trade."

Thirty: The Last Letter

Herewith—April-of-my-life,
the rest of my years.
I loved you the moment I met you,
knees hugged, pensive in that library,
trying to decipher "The War of the Three Kingdoms"
in a poor translation.
What happened to your long black hair
and to your mother language,
simple and sincere:
Sea. Moon. Pearl. Tears.
Your leavetaking begins here.

Marilyn Chin

Beauty, My Sisters, Is Not Regalia

I am no prettier than you
My face is scarred
With reticence, deeply etched
Since childhood. We watched
Our mother sink into the sea
And our father, standing
Under an ailanthus
Gazing
Not at her, but
At the sea.
For the sea is made of knives
And only one man
Can walk over them
(The rest of us are women
Or might as well be).
How can I explain the sea
How it swallows me up
Only to tumble me forth
Over and over . . .
My dress gets wet
And I blame my emotions.
How will I tell you
About him
How we fit
Like mortar and pestle
Snake in a hole, we fit.
Here's a navel, here's a seedless
Here's everything you want in an orange
Here's fulfillment and everything
I meant . . . *Mother*
I am not telling you where
I am going so that
Where I end up will always be
A surprise. The virtue of America
Is that she has no direction.
The problem with Imperial Japan was that
She knew too well
Her direction.
And China's direction
I think
Today
October 30, 1980
Is good.

Marilyn Chin

So Lost in Him

He kissed each of her long fingers
calloused from playing the lute.
She was also learning the samisen then
and even some Western guitar.
Against parents, against
the gossip of sisters,
she played for him
and never again for another.
She strummed, headbent,
looking up only once or twice
into his freshly shaved face
so clean and blue in the moonlight.

In the morning, half way down
toward the tended grove,
bamboo and acacia tangled.
So lost in him, she couldn't feel
the underbush, wet with dew,
soaking her zori and
the hem of her new dungarees,
nor the fawn dying within her.

Marilyn Chin

The End of a Beginning

The beginning is always difficult.
The immigrant worked his knuckles to the bone
only to die under the wheels of the railroad.
One-thousand years before him, his ancestor fell
building yet another annex to the Great Wall—
and was entombed within his work. And I,
the beginning of an end, the end of a beginning,
sit here, drink unfermented green tea,
scrawl these paltry lines for you. Grandfather,
on your one-hundredth birthday, I have
the answers to your last riddles:

This is why the baboon's ass is red.
Why horses lie down only in moments of disaster.
Why the hyena's back is forever scarred.
Why, that one hare who was saved, splits his upper lip,
in a fit of hysterical laughter.

Marilyn Chin

I'm Ten, Have Lots of Friends and Don't Care

The old fat man who lived nearer to the neon clock
came down the fire escape only once a year.
He was ugly like Mr. Wang Wei and even worse,
One day he opened up his red baggy pants and said,
"for you, my children, for you."
And sister and me got to milk his bull.
Five years later, we giggled and knew it was wrong.
He was dead now and we shouldn't "blacken a dead man's eye
    with rocks and lies."
Grandma cursed us for having no heart.
I looked down at my chest and surely she was right.

Sister turns beautiful and moves to the country suddenly.
I'm still ten, have lots of friends and don't care.
Some say the old man died with loneliness and no furniture.
His life certainly didn't fit his name which was "Lucky."
God, but everybody's name is "Lucky," "Healthy," "Joy," or "Money."
Chinese names are all like that.
Except for sister who moved to the country.
She changed it to Rose and Ma hasn't talked to her since.
Grandma spews four-character phrases and I know
I'll never see my sister again.

Marilyn Chin

A Chinaman's Chance

If you were a Chinese born in America, who would you believe,
Plato who said what Socrates said
Or Confucius in his bawdy way:
    "so a male child is born to you
    I am happy, very very happy."

The railroad killed your great-grandfather.
His arms here, his legs there . . .
How can we remake ourselves in his image?

Your father worked his knuckles black
So you might have pink cheeks. Your father
Burped you on the back; why must you water his face?

Your father was happy, he was charred by the sun,
Danced and sang until he died at twenty-one.

Lord, don't you like my drinking. Even Jesus
Had a few in his day with Mary before
He gambled his life for us on the cross—

And for us he lost his life, for us.

Your body is growing, changing, running,
Away from your soul. Look,

Not a sun but a gold coin at the horizon,
Chase after it, my friend, after it.

Why does the earth move backwards
As we walk ahead. Why does mother's
Blood stain this hand-me-down shirt?

This brown of old tea, the yellow ring
Around the same porcelain cup. They stayed

Stone-faced as paired lions, prepared
As nightwatch at the frontier gate.

We have come small and wooden, tanned brown
As oak pillars, eyes peering straight
Through vinyl baggage and uprooted shoes.

We shall gather their leftovers: jimsons and velvets,
Crocuses which have burst-bloomed through walks.
We shall shatter this ancient marble, veined and glorious . . .

Little path, golden arrows, could you pave
My future in another child's neighborhood?

Night: black starred canopy, piece
Of Chinese silk, dank with must and cedar,
Pulled down from the source, a cardboard bolt.

Marilyn Chin

After my last paycheck from the factory,
two thin coupons, four tin dollars,
I invited old Liu for an afternoon meal.

for the Chinese Cultural Revolution
and all that was wrong with my life

I ordered vegetables and he ordered dog,
the cheapest kind, mushu, but without the cakes.
I watched him smack his greasy lips
and thought of home, my lover's gentle kisses—
his faint aroma, still with me now.

I confided with a grief too real,
"This is not what I expected"
and bit my lip to keep from crying,
"I've seen enough, I want to go home."
But suddenly, I was seized by a vision

reminding me why I had come: two girls
in uniform, red bandanas and armbands
shouting slogans and Maoish songs,
"the East is red, the sun is rising;"
promises of freedom and a better world.

Trailing them was their mascot of Youth,
a creature out of Doctor Seuss or Lewis Carroll,
purplish pink, variegated and prancing.
I stood in awe of its godlike beauty
until the realist Liu disrupted my mirage.

"It's the dog I ordered and am eating still!"
he mumbled with a mouthful of wine.
And as it came closer I saw the truth:
its spots were not of breeding or exotic import,
but rampant colonies of scabbies and fleas,

which, especially red in its forbidden country,
blazed a trail through the back of its woods;
and then, its forehead bled with worms,
so many and complex as if *they* did its thinking.
I rubbed my eyes, readjusted the world . . .

Then focused back on his gruesome dish
trimmed with parsley and rinds of orange.
One piece of bone, unidentified which,
stared at me like a goat's pleading eye
or the shiny new dollar I'd just lost.

Old Liu laughed and slapped my back,
"You American Chinese are hard to please."
Then, stuck his filthy chopsticks into my sauce.
"Mmmm, seasoning from Beijing, the best
since opium," then, pointed to a man

sitting behind me, a stout provincial governor
who didn't have to pay after eating the finest
Chinese pug, twenty-five yuan a leg.
He picked his teeth with a splintered shin,
burped and farted, flaunting his wealth.

Old Liu said with wine breath to kill,
"My cousin, don't be disillusioned,
his pride will be molested, his dignity violated,
and he as dead as the four-legged he ate
two short kilometers before home."

Marilyn Chin

A Dream in the Life of American Joe

Soll ich dir, Flammenbilding, weichen?
(Should I, phantom of fire, fly?)
                                    Faust

Sink of dirty dishes, snails crawling on reefs,
My cousin the crustacean hangs by a claw . . .

The wall is long, dull long,
But longer my Tibetan dream-girl's hair.

Was she a whore or wasn't she that imaginative—
Straightlaced as California brine.

2
Four o'clock, favorite highball,
June the Loon plops her dank marten down, wraps
Her leathers around me, fumbles
My prunes, takes me to Mars.

3
Climbing the stairs to "Cold Mountain,"
For the elevator's down.
Climbing the stairs to "Cold Mountain,"
For the elevator's down.
A tall glass awaits, cool, misty, foam on top.
The woman I love is waiting
Sucking a red cherry, a bitter olive,
A pearly onion, salt around the brim.

I said, "Why have you come to 'Cold Mountain?'"
She said, "Baby, do you know who I am?"

4
She is the girl with the queue-rope of black hair,
The girl who brings you Blue Nun and souvenirs
Made in Hong Kong, small bright thingamajigs
That snake from your pelvis to your heart, rigged

With bedroom accoutrement: plush carpeting, Pioneer
        tapedeck;
But in the morning before her shower she's a wreck,

Standing releve in front of the mirror, chanting
    I am the Queen Dowager
    I shall break my nose
and paint on an extra-epicanthic fold.

Pink, violet, blue-haze
How could I have seen through those cloudy days
Or has the world died in my rendering?

5
Insula Peninsula
Daughter of Sangfroid
But she was never beautiful

Black braids holding back the pride
Of lions—a flower sequestered
By bees

Empty, hollow, nugatory
Follow my fugue
This is where you'll find me

Taipei, Chung Shan Pei Road
My head nailed to a giant cross, smoking
A British cigar

6
Again, again the palm trees sway
On the island which they call Kauai.
My girl always a kilometer away, nets fish;
But I have snagged nothing but roughage.
My twentieth century tower—the bridges lit
With a curious string of wonder: birds in a gamut
From high to low; and all they cry is "sky."

7
Spleen of Maui, gall of Taiwan
Two billion Asian women couldn't be wrong

Ideographs, Rapidiographs
Short-lived Mrs. Livingstons, Nancy Kwans

The next stops will be Barbados (oo-la-la)
Samoa, Fiji, Calypso

time to crow

I cannot crow
I do not crow

Just enough to bend a jonquil
The first snow

Marilyn Chin

We Are Americans Now, We Live in the Tundra

Today in hazy San Francisco, I face seaward
Toward China, a giant begonia—

Pink, fragrant, bitten
By verdigris and insects. I sing her

A blues song; even a Chinese girl gets the blues,
Her reticence is black and blue.

Let's sing about the extinct
Bengal tigers, about giant Pandas—

"Ling Ling loves Xing Xing . . . yet,
we will not mate. We are

Not impotent, we are important.
We blame the environment, we blame the zoo!"

What shall we plant for the future?
Bamboo, sasagrass, coconut palms? No!

legumes, wheat, maize, old swines
To milk the new.

We are Americans now, we live in the tundra
Of the logical, a sea of cities, a wood of cars.

Farewell my ancestors:
Hirsute Taoists, failed scholars, farewell

My wetnurse who feared and loathed the Catholics,
Who called out:

    Now that the half-men have occupied Canton
    Hide your daughters, lock your doors!

Marilyn Chin

SHALIN HAI-JEW

The youngest poet in this anthology, Shalin Hai-Jew was born in Alabama in 1965, the second of three daughters to a Chinese immigrant family. Her father is an engineer and her mother an artist. She entered the University of Washington at age 15 as an Early Entrant, and graduated with B.A.s in English and Psychology, and an M.A. in English. She won the 1983 Hugh Paradise Scholarship, 1985 Joan Grayston Award; received a 1985 Ucross Foundation Residency; was one of fifteen 1985 Wesleyan "New Poets Series" finalists; and received the *Columbia* Annual Editor's Prize for Poetry in 1987. Her poetry has appeared in numerous publications. She teaches in the Seattle community college system and writes for Seattle's *International Examiner*.

As I was born and raised in the U.S, the "Chinese" in Chinese-American is an adjective modifying "American." I studied Mandarin briefly, and joined the apolitical Chinese Student Association in college; visited Hong Kong and China in 1983-84; and have written poems and translated children's stories from my parents' oral-Toishanese homeland recollections—to explore and reclaim some of my heritage. I taught at Jiangxi Normal University in Nanchang, Jiangxi Province, China, from October 1988 to June 1990. My experiences there were chronicled in a twice-monthly column in the Seattle Chinese Post titled "The Silver Pot Journals." I hope to live and teach again in China at a future time.

The U.S. provides a strong base for writers. People have access to world class literature, authors and speakers, art, foreign films, an informed and varied news media, a lively writing and publishing community.

Here's to continued good relations between the U.S. and China—cheers!

Interpreting the Scene

(from an untitled photograph by Jane Tuckerman, 1979)

A naked woman leans out the open window,
arms raised in reverence to the light
that hugs her like the damp room, her face, torso,
lost as a body immersed in water.
From where we stand, probably in a doorway,
we see floorboards dank around her feet
where moisture weighted the wood before her.
Darkness a halo in the corners, under
the heater, on the fourth wall beyond sight,
the light, too, is unrevealing. On tiptoe,
does she see what lies below: eight floors
down? a spread of lawn and tulips?
brick? If she turned around, silhouetted,
she could laugh at our stealth, our concern,
trip back into the room seemingly darker,
and empty of chairs and voices. Or not.
We would like to imagine it so. Okay,
there is this woman, and her motive.
A pose. A dare. A joke. Our latter explanations
are ludicrous as this naked woman
halfway over the sill. But then,
there is this light. Like warmth?

Shalin   Hai-Jew

Three Disasters

"Asians believe that everyone must guard against three
disasters in life: fire, thieves, and ghosts."

—Chinese astrology

You pause the pause before confessions
while I trace the yoke of your collarbone,
lift your robe off all the way down
so it catches on your wrists.
The dikes behind your eyes,
are they to contain or deflect?
The mood elusive as first light,
you close me out beyond the beige veil
of your eyelids. I touch you like stroking
raised hairs. If I tip your chin,
your eyes will keep you. Through our maze
we stumble to this place, again. You will wake
from your trance, certain the wish rings
will be lodged on your fingers.
Do you know how many nights
you could have stayed? Do you imagine
I will surround you like fire, pocket
your seed like coins, enter
your sanctuary with the wind?

Shalin Hai-Jew

Kinged

Crumpled like an embroidered pillowcase
on the floor, the old woman cries
in the smouldering of incense and steamed glass.
She is packing to return to Ohio;
her daughter has told her, "Your two years here
are up. You should go back while the weather
is warm." She has found money
as a thumb in sponge cake
leaves little impression. A kinged checker,
she is finally moving backwards
in a history of frontiers; Canton
to Hong Kong to Ohio to Seattle.

She is surprised at how the board
has cleared so quickly, how she can move
and not see another for several turns.
Soil, beyond red and black, flavors the meats,
the sun in her laundry. Only her dreams
recycle, black on gray, gray
going grayer. Her eyes swell
like beans in water, shift up
towards her skull at night.

She wonders how maternal love fails
so utterly that hate can spread like clover,
spread so that her daughter can carve
her out of her grandchildren's lives,
so utterly weeded out. Astonished
at each thump of her heart, she thinks
a piece of her must erode and drift
into her blood for it to be creeping
so slowly now. So red. Black.

Shalin   Hai-Jew

Alliances

Easily persuaded as changing the subject
in conversation, we believe *we are together*
is what matters, though we have broken vows
like branches over our knees, again
and again like an ax coming down. I set
the table, dust the bone china
for tea, to hear out your new adventure.
The boredom that sparks appetite
or deadens sense like hearing
on shifting elevations, has driven you
to play puppet to our minds' wanderings,
both equally sinning. Like a blister
on your instep, the robin we found
under the Chevy hood, we are no longer
surprised at how things happen.
As our marriage putters beyond control,
how careful we are with our bodies
like old linens, that we can feel so little,
the preparations against hunger or cold
so neither enter fully.
We are continually bowing out, no pain
greater than stubbing our toes.
A craving satisfied once—is it enough?
Condemned, you return. Your automatic,
running appeal is granted. Sweet James,
this is meant to last.

Shalin Hai-Jew

This Night

(for J.W.Y.)

Taste of peaked champagne
dry like salt in my throat,
I twist in your hands
and watch the string
of Japanese tissue roses
unfold, a fist of the Issei.
From the open shutters,
pine rustles like broom straw.
We lie still to listen.

In the newborn calm
after a Midwest rainstorm,
when wind-weary cones drop
back on hard soil,
we have fallen.
Air spills like rain over us;
the moment for dreams passes,
untallied. Words pelt heavy
and dissolve into this night
as sumi strokes to wet rice
paper sheaths. We huddle
like children saving warmth.

High tide stealing sand
from under our feet,
we pull closer. But the end
was written before we turned
page one, lines scribed
on open palms. I recall
your laughter, your voice,
until the silence
becomes a noise.
You roll away.

Shalin   Hai-Jew

How to Read the Poem She Wrote for You

for R.T.

Shade this love poem over with pencil
for an outline: a breast.
A goblet. Read it, Roy,
like a riddle, an anecdote, or consider it
seriously as you would an article.
Let it ferment for a month, then snap
open like a can of biscuits. Shake it;
something may fall out: a bookmark,
splat of wine. Turn it on your frayed knee
patch; fold this page into a boat or plane.
Watch it float and fly. Press
it under ultra-violet light or water.
Tap it. It may spit
out a pebble, a pit, a pearl.
Splay your fingers into a rake
and let the words tumble like rice
onto them. Drop this onto concrete
or stand it up on end
to see which way it falls.

All two hundred and sixty-eight pieces
are here, revealing
what the poet has decided your fate
is to be. She draws you in the shapes
she finds pleasing, makes fiction
to suit her. Reading her poem
may be like looking at your face
in a carnival mirror, for she will show
angles from blind spots,
reveal places where your skin is soft
as an eyelid, rough as her tongue,
show you in cellar light or make up
dialogue for you like a lie,
"Anna. Anna."

Start reading by bracing yourself
against her back door. If you find
her poem empty as an urn,
with words missing or misspelled,
flat as poured champagne,
stretching out like a couch, then go
to her, Roy. She will tell you.

Shalin Hai-Jew

Comfort for a Muse

for R. T.

This is home though he's stayed away a year.
      He undresses while she waits with paints, inks,
         to recreate him.
Her son suckles clumsily; milk dribbles.
      She's magically borne another man's child
         while he circled.
It's no consolation that he's her sole muse,
      that posterity belongs to her who's loved him,
         that she credits him by name,
that some of their collaborations will last beyond
      a human life. His freedom is absolute as sky—
         to find love as a full shell
among rocks, father children like kites to let soar,
      make a wife from any number of lovers.
         He could leave, knowing
a muse bears a kind of fertility. Yet,
      she's irreparably typecast him, refused
         to acknowledge his grief. He poses
with his hands out to protest the men
      who've cluttered her bed like newspapers.
         He holds his groin to mourn the infinite
seeds mixed in sand. He crouches like a beggar
      to symbolise her neglect. He points to accuse her
         of betraying her *self*. He shakes
his fists at life continuing around their stasis,
      like water around a rock. He circles his arms
         to show her absence.
Monkey with an audience, he rocks an imaginary cradle.
      Then, stops. She knows.
         "Sam," she says. He rests his head
on her bony, sodden lap.

Shalin   Hai-Jew

JASON HWANG

The poet Jason Hwang is by profession a musical composer and performing artist (violin). He has performed his music in Germany, Holland, numerous Kool Jazz Festivals and has been featured by Voice of America Radio. He has written many film scores and has performed/recorded with leading musical thinkers. As a poet he has given reading performances (utilizing spoken and recorded poetry, percussion and violin) at various galleries and colleges; co-edited the anthology *American Born and Foreign: An Anthology of Asian American Poetry*, published by the poetry magazine *Sunbury*, and was chosen by Poetry in Public Places to have his work appear on thousands of New York City buses. In addition, Mr. Hwang is the director of *Afterbirth*, a poetic documentary film exploring the cultural predicament of American-born Chinese. *Afterbirth* was presented by the Museum of Modern Art and the Public Broadcasting System.

Creative questions are difficult to analyze because writing poetry or music is an intuitive process for me. Instinct guides me from one word to the next, sound after sound. I attempt to cultivate faith in individualism, striking a personal balance between my "animalism" and intellect. There can be no self-consciousness toward textbook rules or critics if words, images and sounds are to be dealt with directly. An honest approach to the creative process will create life-like poems infused with the power of originality. Now that's a challenge!

myself
the arriving presence listened
and greeted the gathering
an afterbirth
revealing untold gestures rippling
across the depths as
a chorus unfurled
surging through
the unseen dimensions
coiled layer upon layer,
a seashell
like an ear
sifting through the sandy curves
the resonance
composed of minute folds the
creased sandpaper
polishing the stones gathered on shore
a party soothed by earth music
a song on harsh surfaces
a miraculous wash of prehistory.
I stand close to where my father has stood
footprints brushed on to the beach with dark blue ink
a lyric notation
of a joyous reunion.

Jason Hwang

does something have to die or breakaway
for growth, progress
say
an arm must be cut off for
her feet to grow into her mother's sandals
or be bared to the holes in her own shoes, which pinch and hurt.

Bound feet used to be attractive.

But can you love and be unable to run
never stopping to see the footprints
the shape of lips, of a kiss
on the sand, on the forest earth,
the past.

Loving and hoping.

And without her arm, her mother's sandals became worn on the edges,
walking at a tilt, the small heel beveled to the motion of an old person's
rocking chair
I, who was your arm, loved you as you sliced the flesh through our shoulder
and wore the edges of your mother's blood, I broke off my feet
and moved away.

Now when we meet on the streets, we are both older,
grown we think
walking like the shape of a rocking chair and we
stop
occasionally
to glance at our footprints
On the sand, on the forest earth
in our hearts.

Jason Hwang

cloud torn by its silent image
bliss gently rolling through drowning grass
skin surfacing through bath waters awaiting
the storm in the faint green light
numerous strands murmur over their
gradual loss of will, turning
over in the disturbance, wrenching each desire
into a blur
a restless movement from center to edge
leaving us blank   and   tense
cold skin
sharp moisture wrapping its transparency
over dreams, a grassy field and
no sound escapes.
It's a lens magnifying
shapes without light.
the reflection slowly torn as
it sits on the water's edge
no sound escapes.

Jason Hwang

uncountable
the marks left by fish
flocking to the reef
with boneless arms,
(elegant gestures for an offering)
a slow resistance in our sleep
beige clouds approach a blue darkness

Evening turning the night,
the wrinkle of
sheets rising with
each breath
together and apart shifting
into the shapes of islands,
each pause
defying the current.

On the sand
holding each other
our sleep forms a
boneless imprint
in the sea
wrapping ourselves, barely visible
under a sheet of eloquent alternations,
gestures flocking to our
rippling outline
which will not erode . . .

again and again
a slow approach
the offering, countless and accepted
(asleep we are ancient)
into our arms,
an island
a veil
a graceful, steadfast motion.

Jason Hwang

without breath

as I run through the forest
   sun flashes like a magnificent flag through the branches
     air in ripples
       enter my lungs like falling leaves
         floating fragrance
          stills my mind
            which becomes who i was
            the motion who i am

i run until
   wind plows the flesh, a current of wrinkles the
    skin between brows of pine

and my legs run without and
ran.

aged sunlight
traveling far
and with great speed
appears still
young as the leaves bursting into flames as they fall
continuous

memory

                                  Jason Hwang

Commencement

A turn of the wrist
palm facing the earth, a delicate eclipse of warmth
face tilting the sky in sunlight
a spokeless wheel   in unison
small gestures fill the room with unseen movement. Like wind.
We are touched. We spin
A dance gracing earth.
Sweeping strokes of air, precious
Reach to embrace
When we love

Jason Hwang

ALEX KUO

Alex Kuo was born in Boston in 1939. He received his B.A. from Knox College in 1961 and M.F.A. from the University of Iowa in 1963, both in creative writing. He has been teaching writing in various universities in the United States and currently lives in Moscow, Idaho. His first collection *The Willow Tree* was published in 1971, as one of the first solo poetic publications by a Chinese American poet. His other works were collected in *New Letters from Hiroshima and Other Poems* (1975) and *Changing the River* (1986). Beside poems, Alex Kuo has also written short stories, essays and book reviews. Since 1974, he has been the literary editor of *The Journal of Ethnic Studies*. He was awarded a National Endowment for the Arts Fellowship in fiction in 1990, and a Fulbright in 1991-92.

I write when I can. There are no boundaries. The definition is in each word and moment, and the line does not form to the right.

Politicking and networking are powerful forces in publishing contracts, grant awarding, and major reading invitations, with the racist establishment circles but equally real within our small ethnic-, Asian-, and Chinese-American literary communities. I have tried to avoid these scenes, and I believe the price I've paid has been less.

Dream Lake, Idaho

My mouth is surrounded
I am thirsty in my own country
My sleeves turn dark and open out

At the edge of the pier
The beach ends and is mapped back
To the edge of the parking lot

There are figures along the beach
Where the fog has let them through
Their raincoats keep them from leaving

But nothing is about to happen
There is the wind and here is the rain
So far they have meant nothing

I listen in silence
And refuse nothing from my cup
This lake will not come by once more

Alex Kuo

Winter Kill

It begins
with parchment of aspen
and it is grief
drifting in early arrival.

 It is more than think:
a deer skull a rabbit's
winter coat the thicket
of spruce cones a boar's
tooth the lynx's skulking
and the suffering quail
the sun's escarpment and
the mind's winter coping
the summer tick.

Do not believe it less
than late.

And it ends
with the idea of pain
slicing up the deep cold
without eyes.

Look at it
look at it falling
from the alphabet.

Alex Kuo

At Wolf Creek Pass, Colorado

, where water cuts
and divides granite

neurotic like the collusion
of former loves tucked

away in this postcard
of the aspen groves

it is loosely obligatory
the existential Kodak

learning a conceit:
always getting away

in my car
and driving

away from the disaster
on roads snowed under

most of the year
short of trust

in this cold, cobalt
air. Away

from the bottom
of the photograph, it is

indisputably only
water, two parts

hydrogen, one oxygen
starting its 12,000 feet
descent: here
I frame what I can

with every
conceivable reason.

Alex Kuo

Coming Home

1

It is vaguely hibiscus
from home, or banyan.
It is you
taking me in
deep from winter river
at low, cold water.
And it is you
shuddering imperceptibly
from our confession
until we are
both surrounded
by the drifting
of this clear, root water
in our confluence.

2

   I was born going
away, and I have
done what I have done
the alphabet always immaculate
and the departures
frequent and convincing
but somehow merciful.

In spring the water will darken
and rise, disappearing again
into absolution.
I will thicken my roots
and extend them
to your secret water.

It will be for us deeper.

3

It is
the poem that forgives.

So do not bother now
to look for me
elsewhere then
for I have
become the trust
that surrounds you
refusing to let go.
And until I can
put your name on my tongue
hold on
to this silence
and believe it home.

Alex Kuo

Did You Not See

the aspens yesterday
intolerant and drawn
together high up on the Divide?

Perhaps you gave them a glance
gazing out the high window
in the back of your house
saw nothing and now
remember nothing more?

What did the second settlers
see when they first stumbled
up these yellowed tiers
trying to find their way to
the Pacific, their senses drying
in that October trying
to change their significance?

Perhaps now you can remember
their prints in that early ice
how they packed along their dead
until the ground was soft
enough for late burial
step after step
disappearing high into
this incomprehensible blue.

Alex Kuo

The River

We live by it, bank deep
By choice near where some ducks
Have also come to believe
This fierce geography that the wind
Will not forget in the next change.

We live in it, in its echo
That is a question, and what it asks
Is a breath forming its words
There on the opposite century, here
On this seemless shore, this abundance.

One year I followed it back
To its beginning in a glacial gap
The next night all the seasons moved
A half moon over my head rising
At last released from all counting.

We live for it, in its story
Dispersed as we are flesh in its eddies
Of meaning, this wider water
And its settlement among leaves
Glittering with teeming assertion.

We live like this, our breath
Over the river's edge, reason
Collecting at the changing waterline
Where only a vague mark forms
Between promise and possibility.

Alex Kuo

Andrew Jackson & The Red Guards

Behind their championship
Lies the game of life

Mercenaries coached to win
Everything in sight

After the season's final game
They left on tour

Exhibition matches
In every remote village

You've seen them, all
Stars on Monday night TV

Led by the Gang of Four
And those cheerleaders

From China's Shan Shi Province
Viciously stupid and bland

Cucumber legs churning up power
As far away as Tibet

Where some still remain
As local bullies

One of them actually
Endorsed his chopsticks

And became the seventh president
Of the United States.

Alex Kuo

A Chinaman's Chance

Shanghai, *1945*

When the bombs dropped on us at the end of the war
No one knew which side did it. We were under
Blankets, beds, that inside table, even chairs

Later when I walked out of the dropzone, I counted
The steps that were not mapped at the beginning
Wanting everyone to have the same, necessary things

Hundreds were queued up on every street corner
For airdropped powdered milk, chocolate, condoms
By the same planes that dropped the bombs the night before

If the truth be known, I had to kill to get away
Lucky, as luck would have it, I wasn't born
In the 18th century: Mozart loved slurs then

For heroes now, I retain Clemente, Gould, my two sons
And what the wind leaves: they have been here
All this time nearer my life, nearer my starfield

For direction, I call on the far points
That insist at intervals without explanation
That left with me in the last, unmarked C-46

Like that last flight out of Casablanca in 1940
In the fog and at gunpoint, just like that
Shutting out of a life, leaping out past the finish

Do not mistake me or look for me in another meaning
Where I won't be found. In a sense we have all survived
Our words depend on it, with each chance

Alex Kuo

The Picture

1

Preface

O Peggy, Peggy! wherefore art thou Peggy?

Whatever happens, I am ready with my eye. It is my first eye that sees, but when I want to remember, I use the camera to hold it forever.

*

Have you ever sat down and thought about the camera? How it turns an innocent moment into an exhibition, something we don't want to have happened, or be seen in that way. However it is recorded in that one moment, someone will always be keeping an eye on it, even when they are not looking at it, like the picture hanging in your bedroom.

*

But let me tell you also about betrayal. It is always there, that lie between the moment and the picture, since we rarely find in it what we foolishly want to record. The instant we look at the picture, we know something's been betrayed and what we're looking at is something entirely different from what we want to remember.

Sometimes this betrayal is physical, like a blemish or a slight hitch of a leg in anticipation, which we only notice or regret in retrospect. When we know that someone else is also looking at us in this same way, we involuntarily begin to make allowances for it, and since then nothing is ever seen as truthfully.

Othertimes it is purely spiritual, like leaving the church the way we have learned to leave home or children or companion to live in a separate pain far away, the way Monet walked into the 20th century on lily pads, barely paying any attention to the details.

*

Some will even say that this is where one's real life begins, after we have stepped away and betrayed our confidences.

*

But mostly what's seen in the picture comes a little bit too late, and then we have the echo of catching up to the tedium and swamp of everyday living, the difference between plateau and surf.

2

The camera they bought with change saved over several months was first kept for weeks at his apartment, then at hers even though they don't sleep without the other, haven't since they started saving money together. It went where he or she went, whomever it was with that day, and wherever they were to spend the night. But being forgetful, sometimes they would be without it, left at his or her other place. At such times they would be helpless at sex, feeling something missing in their lives. The last time this happened sleepless at three in the morning, they thumped out of bed into his car and drove through flashing yellow traffic lights to the other side of town to her apartment in record time. In the clarity of those two hours waiting for the sunrise, they discussed if the first roll of film into the camera should be black-and-white or color, Japanese or German, since it was made in one country with the other's optics. That was the morning they also decided that the camera should be kept at her apartment, since they are more often together there—that way they'll always know where it is, even if they're not there by mistake. This is the way reason prevails, and why we suck on each other's tit. You better believe it.

3
Lives in Dreadful Wanting

Then they are young and on vacation, their camera out snapping pictures of each other in front of the fountain.

They are by the seashore with their camera.

They are at the foot of the alps with their camera.

Wherever they are away from home, their story is twice told.

They are in each other's pictures looking out, one of them always smiling, but we are never sure which one and when.

You just look great, smile.

I want to get this just right.

He waves her to the left, she waves him to the right. They wave at each other wherever they are.

A little closer. Closer, still. Come on, closer.

There. Snap, click, shutter getting in between two actions.

*

Several actions later, there are children. First, one in blue in mother's arms, on a Sunday outing in the park, then several digressions later in trimmed white sweater holding father's hand, he is old enough not to want to be in the picture, displaced by sister in pink in mother's arms, whose soul has not moved since the last picture was snapped. They are no longer smiling and waving.

When the prints came back from Fotomat the next day, there was too much light, they said, the camera too close for allowances, and what it captured was not what they wished, but someone else keeping an eye on them.

We should save up and buy another camera, they said together under a Christmas tree one year.

4

Nothing is ever the same as they said it was.
D. Arbus

I told her that it said when you can't get close enough to your subject you must shoot from a distance, but she wanted to read the pamphlet for herself.

This is just what I thought, she said.

I asked what that was, but I knew they weren't the right words even before I said them.

You don't have to, she said.

What's that?

Telephoto.

What's that? What telephoto?

You don't need to be up close. You don't need to. You can stand up high on a cliff and get a detailed picture of the sandy beach way below you.

With a telephoto lens, I see.

That's what I said, she said, letting all her hair down, not a cow-eyed shuffling gal of the earth, but a belle of the cradle since birth.

*

Now there are the children, one in blue, and one in pink. Their parents are ambivalent toward their lives and sometimes pass you on the street or sit next to you in a restaurant unnoticed. Sometimes they wish their children away.

Do you want the one in pink, or the one in blue?

5

Words Most Often Mispronounced in Fiction

In bars 21 and 23 of the *Aria* to his "Goldberg Variations," J.S. Bach designated a clear three note ascending slide ornamentation, from the German *Schleifer*, not anticipating that centuries later pianists would be reproducing them with mortal narcissism.

*

How the desire to fall into your lover's arms must be insolent without the threat of loss.

*

It's leaning toward pulse, in even sequences and held at bloodpoint for just a moment to let light in before the letting go, descending in either direction but end at the beginning of the same note turned upside down. You have never been this way before, baby.

*

DEFINITION

I have changed my mind. In my mouth are words that can walk right into the narrative and keep an eye on you.

Do you like these things? Do you wish them? That yellow lamp that lets in the light, this Hasselblad that's seen World War II, or the woman with the mouth of her body open standing by the piano, car keys in hand? She's 33, a violinist who's never killed anyone or taught high school, who last appeared in *Tender is the Night*. Does she fit your needs? You can call her anything you want, except Desperate Innocence.

There, stand closer to her while I snap a picture of the two of you while there's still enough light.

*

Whatever happens, I am ready.

6

*The difference between what belongs and what doesn't
is the ability to balance between plateau and surf.*
L. Sebring

Before daylight I am eager for rain. In my half-sleep the stream
fills with furious birds. There is no electricity to speak of, so the water
flows from top left to bottom right. There are no waves. By six
swimmers exhaust the beach. Someone looks up and takes notes. With
each new sentence something is repeated, some color restored,
something unseen stirs between plateau and surf.

A figure steps out to the edge. She is taking a chance considering
how exaggerated she looks.

A figure steps out to the edge. She is taking a chance, considering
she might be a fugitive hiding from the camera since childhood.

Everything in the center is caught in someone's eye in the same
quantity. The light behind me cannot escape, though the space between
us depends on how far I am willing to walk. How easily I forget that
there is no trail to the vertical except the one I forgive. In daylight it
is every mapmaker's relief. The lines turn outward and balance against
legend. What belongs and what doesn't is the difference in elevation.

Away from the children and the picnickers, the figure at the edge
has not stirred. What belongs here and what doesn't is a difference in
seeing. Love me, love me, in this interval waiting. The space between
us dips, and I lean over to her side at just the right moment and take her
by the nipple. Anything is possible, she says. Our collusion thickens
and branches to blood. The heart fills quickly, leaving no necessity for
metaphor. Only the wind arches, and what it brings has not ceased
since it began.

*

Sometimes I look down there and watch it going back in, retaining as
much as possible. It is all here, without fiction and without question.
There is no pause to name it.

Alex Kuo

ALAN CHONG LAU

Alan Chong Lau was born in California. He received his B.A. in art from the University of California, Santa Cruz. His poetic works, which have appeared in many magazines and anthologies, are collected in *Buddha Bandits Down Highway 99* (1978) and *Songs for Jadina* (1980). In 1982 he served as co-editor for the anthology *Turning Shadows Into Light: Art and Culture of the Northwest Early Asian/Pacific Community*. Most recently he co-edited a special Asian American poetry issue of *Contact II* magazine. He is the recipient of a number of awards, including a grant from the California Arts Council and a Creative Artist Fellowship for Japan.

poems filled with dogma that stomp across the page or those polished to a fine sheen yet so light they float—these prolif-erate and bloom all year around bright and plentiful. The real stuff stays close to the ground, buried in the weeds. Bright moments! Bright moments! Bright moments!

a search for taiping ghosts

for dale and norm kaneko

1

like a blind boy
not sure of destination
get off at every stop
to buy postcards
pasting them in a book of days

wind sea grass fire leaves
these form the other pages

if i were like others
i would be home now
instead blow
on a flute of bones
comforted by the sound

at night a path of light
crosses the river
taiping ghosts scurry over
melt into the gleam of blood red cliffs

i want to follow
but the boatman is afraid
to move the oar
"no one passes the tatu at night"

we sit in his hut
recalling the broken names
of our country's heroes

"have you heard of those
who defaced the altars
turned over the incense urns
drove coughing scholars out in smoke?"

he spits
piercing the head of a nail
above the washboard
nods as the moon nudges his head

"i have seen so many skeletons on the road
no longer can i sleep at night
have you seen those skeletons walking?"

2

i love to hear the birds
sing the sun up
night's finger nails
carry the blood
of too many lice cracked in corners

daylight's fingers
are soft drumming mallets
of gold

lugging a watermelon to a village
i wear a hat of leaves
juicy thoughts plunder
my mind of any silence

last time i saw a woman
she had bells on her ankles
they sang as she ran
thru tall grass swishing

my thoughts on this
and i can't help but stumble
in the distance a waterwheel
sings of its own accord
tongues of water

the book i am writing
is full of postcards
addresses of vendors orphans barefoot peasants
people who don't exist

wind sea grass fire leaves
these form the other pages

Alan Lau

ashes and food

1

ashes
    only dust
    fine fragrant ashes
    incense

presented
lit
cast and returned

stir it
into mud
after a rain

the colour

soft but solid
swirls
undulating wisps of shadow
burning earth

2

grandmother . . . today
clear enough
to breathe in the ashes
of last night's stars

sun
hot enough
to break bones
starts with skin first

drops of
sweat
lance outward
and come out colourless
clear

already cars
heading home
look for the road

clouds of brown dust cover
the chicken
we leave you

Alan Lau

the promise

for sharon lew and the first, second,
third and all generations to come . . .
workers of the soil, all children
of the land

1

my grandfather
detained
on an island
of hell named angel

"from your backdoor
how many feet
is the village pond?
in what direction
does your house
lie in relation to it?"

    —immigration authority questions

your parents
contained
up here in the *original* tules
where it still snows
in april
streaks of white
on engulfing crags of stone

here where man
is a pin
and silence replaces the scream
of anger once righteous enough
to bring tanks grumbling to
the barbed front door

your used barracks
are rented out to new prisoners
migrant workers
who stoop over to pick
the dark mud from their shoes
as geese draw the distance
between peaks

here on an island
of sun bleached rocks
where chinese grandmothers
sat on benches
in the long afternoon
waiting years feet inches
for entrance to gold mountain
the broken glass of windows
lay on the floor
jagged tears eating dust

green thriving bushes
cover walls where inside
poems of despair
ten thousand washed out dreams
are scrawled in bitter blood
as sea gulls cut white patterns
in blue sky

today we rode in chartered buses
to get here
with scant belongings as
your parents once rode in buses
bayonets at every window
like a road sign

a former internee
speaks
"this is the first time
i've been here in . . . . ."

(eyes scan
tarpaper walls
counting up time spent
a collapsed guardtower
points to the mountains)

"thirty years . . . . .
it's been . . ."

(the wind cuts us all
to silence
as he no longer
can find words)

today
i take a ferry
across the water
with only a sack lunch
as my grandfather
carried only a bundle wrapped in cloth
tossed in the hold of a ship
like a wet mop

the words on the walls speak
"deprived of my freedom, i stay on this island.
the story of my life is bleached—ending up
in prison.
my breast is full of grievances and this poem
is an outlet." *

2

we come in
all of us with names
not numbers
and

no . . . . .
we will never
go to tule lake again

and no . . . . .
i cannot tell you how many feet
the duckpond is from my backdoor

and no . . . . .
we will never
give up our names

and yes . . . . .
this land is our land

and yes . . . . .
we will share it with
people of all tribes

and yes . . . . .
all your guns
are worthless

and yes . . . . .
it is the same with your empty words

the earth will eat them
will split them
like pulling off the heads
of rusty nails

Alan Lau

*translated by the oakland museum from original poems found etched
into the walls of angel island, a detention center for entering
immigrants in san francisco

wild potatoes *

jump a stone fence
ancestors built
years before

muddy currents oozing silt
water skipper characters
on a glimmer

take off the shoes
dig dig deep
deep underneath rushes
you smell
whenever they burn the delta
out

even without light
grandma can still pick out
the tenderest green shoots

water just soaks cuffs
alone in darkness
we move to the hum of mosquitoes

the occasional moan of a train
in the distance

Alan Lau

*This is the second part of the poem entitled "2 stops on the way home"

Water that Springs from a Rock

*The worst massacre of Chinese happened in Rock Springs, Wyoming, a
coal mining center along the Union Pacific Railroad. On the morning of
September 2, 1885, a number of Chinese were wounded while trying to reason
with white vigilantes bent on excluding all Chinese laborers. After an anti-
Chinese meeting held on the "Whitemen's Town" side of Rock Springs, the
looting and massacre of Chinese began in deadly earnest. Within a few days,
over 28 Chinese were found brutally murdered, and many others seriously
wounded. Property damage numbered in the thousands of dollars.*

From *Chinese Working People in America*
by Wei Min She Labor Committee

(What follows is a fictional account of one victim of the Rock Springs
massacre whose body was never found:)

the settlement resembled the remains of a collapsed accordion
each shelter the haphazard moan of notes taking root where they
     landed
it was as if the contents of a civilization had been particles
tossed from a huge pepper box unto an unmarked space
the impulsive grab for shelter fanning out into homestead and shack
streets were unheard of
when the miners trudged to and from the mines
they formed winding paths of movement that rivaled anthills
today a stranger still gets lost

the smell of chicken ranches after rain
their walls sag along the highway
as if blasts of wind and the retreating momentum
of cars passing by in the night could blow them down
clusters of section houses hug the railroad for company
a highway cuts through sandstone hills bled red into white
from a timeless exposure to the elements
here prehistoric seas left sediments in swirls of waves
when the green river floods in winter
matchsticks of deserted track jam its mouth
a smear of smoke from trains and railroad shops
hangs over the valley on a cloudy day
waiting for rain
in the schoolyard three swings describe the wind

the coal is semi-bituminous
brown coal of good quality
its quantity is practically unlimited
     —1874 Uinta County commissioner

SEEDS IN THE WIND:
FROM THE DIARY OF A RAILROAD WORKER

July 3rd 1885

after working on the railroad
we drifted down to wyoming territory
my brother and i
he barely 20 and i, 25 had survived harsh winters
digging under tunnels of snow
lowered in baskets
we chipped holes in granite cliffs
setting dynamite
that tore a road out of sheer rock
many of our friends died
when fuses were mistimed
or chips of stone blew unexpectedly strong
their cries could be heard for miles
as they fell to the valley below
at times we all had the same nightmares
the sound of their cries echoing in our sleep
gave us little rest
vultures and eagles followed us all the way to Utah
till the track was laid

september lst 1885

in the summer the union pacific shipped us
from evanston to rock springs
to work the coal mines

conditions here
are no better
the white miners resent our presence
open flames are used for light
and fire and explosions
are frequent

coal dust particles
finer than snow
envelope the air
coat our lungs with silt
and making it hard to see

in winter we work in water
10 to 12 hours a day
walk home with fingers of ice
clinging to our legs

the bosses
only want black money
our lives mean nothing
if we get hurt
they just get someone else

september 2nd 1885

my brother lee and i worked on different shifts
one early september found me in the mines
lee stayed at home working on a 100 foot dragon
that when done would require 30 to 40 men to carry thru
    the streets

it was a slow day in the shaft
we hit nothing but rock for a week
visibility was poor
we sat down and had tea
old man wong farted so loud we all had to laugh
chong told him to keep it down or he'd cave us all in
wong went to piss but we kept talking
he never returned

shots sounding like firecrackers
came from the mouth of the mine
for an instant we saw a hand
throw something in the air
an explosion ripped the shaft to pieces
as the screams of miners echoed in smoke
luckily i was furthest away from the blast
i crawled out of the rubble
and ran for a secret exit that led to the sandhills

our men
some still with shovels poured out of the mines
the white demons stayed at a distance in groups
and poured bullets on us like rain
i saw wing and a few others try to defend themselves
swinging shovels but most were cut down
before they could reach their assailants

soon the plains were dotted with bodies
those who could
ran for the sandhills and the desert
the landscape blurred blue and red with our movement

laughing
wives of some miners
took torches to buildings in chinatown
soon the roar of flames shook the street
the sick and wounded were consumed in the heat
or killed as they ran out in swirls of flame
i never saw my brother lee again

september 7th 1885
escape to green river sholes
(last entry)

i have been down
here for a week now
wondering what to do

along this river
are fossil beds
thin crust of colors
line the rocks

the record of life
is kept here
thousands of rainbow hued fish
who poured thru sweet water
a variety of insects
i've never seen before
even in china
the patterns of plants
caught still in their growth
in sunlight
their impressions
cast here for centuries
tell stories of a world
before we ever came

i wish i could take
it all
pour it into shadows
of light
keep it in a box
where i could live
in peace

at night here
i share the stream
with the scurry of prairie dogs
the flicker of eyes in moonlight
owls watch over me
we're all here to escape
the blistering heat
of the sandhills and the hunter

my wounds
add color to the water
as i drink
looking up at this blanket
of stars
i wonder what brought me here

(from governor warren's report
november 25th 1885
u.s. documents, serial #2379)

scores of bodies lined the plains

our blood washed in water licks dust flecked with gold

exhumed from ashes

our bones snap back a rhythm clacked in the spokes of wheels

earth caving in houses

our sweat waters weeds the color of rust in moonlight

the cries and steam of families roasted and buried alive

our screams define the ritual of storm

not a living chinaman—man, woman, or child—was left in the town,
where 700 to 900 had lived the day before

resilient
we grow and thrive in wind
misshapen pods, spores, pollen
living things that take root in sky
and take names like blue   green   yellow   brown

the stench of death followed the railroad east and west

and so we persist
our trestles
veins that tie into roadsigns marking our trail

at the mouth of mines they poured out half naked

our skeletons buried forever become shrines, holy places choked with
weeds and wildflowers

killed as they ran to the sandhills

ribbons of smoke smeared the wyoming sky
it poured a black rain for days and days
but after all everything continued to grow

rock springs bicentennial

After the Rock Springs massacre in 1885 and order was restored, all of the Chinese left Evanston. The little Chinatown decayed, and there were no further New Year's celebrations. As part of the nation's bicentennial Uinta County recreated a Chinese New Year celebration. Residents dressed in oriental garments during the festivities, and Chinese music was played in the downtown area. The windows were decorated with Chinese art and antiques. Fireworks, floats, puppet shows, the parade of the dragon and rickshaw races wound through Rock Springs. Chinese food and fortune cookies were sold to onlookers. It was one of the most exciting programs during the Wyoming bicentennial year.

—The Wyoming History News
January 1977

Alan Lau

CAROLYN LAU

Born and raised in Hawaii, Carolyn Lau came to California and received her M.A. degree from San Francisco State University. After graduation she worked for the gestalt therapist Frederick S. Perls. Though she started to write poetry early, she did not become an active writing poet until she began a serious study of Chinese philosophy. Her poems have appeared in *The American Poetry Review, Hawaii Review, ZYZZYVA*, and other magazines. Her first collection *Wode Shuofa* (My Way of Speaking) was printed by Tooth of Time Books. Carolyn Lau is the recipient of several awards, including a 1989 American Book Award and a California Arts Council Fellowship in Literature. After teaching literature and writing in Tianjin, China, to university students for a year and researching the Secret Women's language in Hunan Province, Lau continues to teach poetry to bilingual immigrant Chinese and other Asian children as an Artist-in-Residence through the California Arts Council.

If a line must be balanced to catch fish,
I will be the line because I am the fish.

　　　—from my poem "Mencius Fulfilled by Escher"

Re-incarnate Blake, Winter 1986

for T

During January rain,
children chase butterflies and
leap into ice that smells like meadow.

Crossing borders, they meet
a small bush that makes sense of loss.

Music, breath engaging
lions, their sun-teeth dripping
wings and shoulder bones of lambs
sing, "heart."

How the lungs drive to love
winter, its better feast, rain.
Give the body eyes, they cry.
"Get out."

Carolyn Lau

Daphne Returning

We were talking about something.
Words rowing in unfamiliar tones
while seagulls lifted me to a corner
of window; the grey paint bordering sky
and Sunday sun touching the bed.

What were we saying? I said it to myself
several times. Separate. Simple.
I was excited lying next to you
even though I didn't kiss a lot
or smile. The moment was big
and steady. My heart was dancing and walking.
The syllables arrived without reason
and left me, new.

Carolyn Lau

Trying to Explain My Fear of Failure
In Terms of the Word "Xiang"
Meaning "To Want, To Think, To Miss"

Once, what his heart saw
while perched on a tree
matched the sun's light.

The tree was still.
Black-and-whiteness etched
a hand on his eye.

Wind and water swept his breath.
Word by word, he rooted earth
adding birds, singing.

Carolyn Lau

In Hades

I walk into my backyard
knowing something about Death:
flowers that shade my hearing.

All year making myself bride,
I pull honeysuckle to my arms as if
enough were not enough. Like Persephone
mixing them in the kitchen with nasturtiums
on the blue and white tablecloth in the sunlight.

All words, these hands have touched,
greedy for what lasts, is confused by the evident:
new breasts for my daughter.
Painting peeling.
Nobody covering it up.

Carolyn Lau

A Footnote to a Dispute
among Confucius's Disciples

The second time my daughter moved
from my house to her father's,
I wrapped myself in a box
to enjoy an end soon coming.

Watching Freud like a stone
that never was The Great Wall,
bundles of nerves spit at
death in its a priori.

As I harvest self by sun and moon
with listening and writing as my tools
dare I test
the men who construct and measure earth?

Wife or not, I turn to look at
what was right
before my breath.

The birds instruct me in the art
to follow senses known at birth.

Carolyn Lau

One Meaning of Dao

For Harriet

I spread from the bottom of mountain

inside tree. Giving the valley

echo. Everyday, the river of

steady sail, permitting

desire. All my body grows flower

as feed for children, as if

I am a most important thing on earth.

Carolyn Lau

Being Chinese in English

August, 1986

The man in the night reading by lamplight.
Nearby, the men playing checkers.

All the varieties of crickets; nervous, cringing.

The balcony gardens insisting
we not, show
while chasing. Orgasm.

Outside, babies questioning their ears; therefore,
shifting twilight upside down
in softspots.

Dear Ox, how desperate we are,
certain only in this thing we can call ours
urging life to feel so good in pleasure.

Carolyn Lau

Regarding Zhuangzi

In August, I won two bells of luck and
kissed Guanyin's white peach cheeks.

Twilight, yesterday, while returning home,
was it her hand that spread across my eye, or
shadows of one half of me?
O mouth that eats a girl in one house;
Fists that beat another somewhere else,
How a mother travelling gathers how and
laughs at dawn each white hair!

O father of my inner ear,
master of the arts-mind,
is it a lie to call life Good?

Can he be me who volleys questions and desires?

Carolyn Lau

Translating "Man" from Chinese into Californian

Maybe: Obsessed with sex and science,
                The eyes tilted, hiding from green light,
                how a mouth matches sound
                laughs and scratches something inside me.

                Fearless, Number One,
                scholar waits-on life:
                body after body gambles all
                to mend and create new cracks in dream.

Maybe not, of course: Again, the car and sun;
                               nectarines and summer feel
                               without. The impulse to stop
                               in the middle. Scoops
                               breast or cock
                               echo-la-la-ing
                               shifts in sculpture.
                               Cool. Tan and muscles lying
                               in my dress, slicings
                               of our sunny-rose flavors.

                                             Carolyn Lau

Footloose among Fourth Century Sophists or

Discovering Ah Q in Ourselves

"Woman" is longer than "man".

An arrow makes no sense:
In my body, your tips move;
in yours, no.

Half a stick, Ah Q.
stick half in little nun.

A cut braid and silver peach.
A chopped head upon a stick

Wooden bars form a grating
with three walls,
there's room.

Bend the wind into your pocket.
Sell and sing a line before too late!

Carolyn Lau

Six Versions of Qiu Jin

Qiu Jin (1875-1907) was China's first feminist martyr. Despite her independent nature, she managed to remain married to the dandified son of a wealthy landlord who was chosen by her family.   To the astonishment of those in the capital, she asked for and received the first divorce granted to a woman in Chinese history.

When Dr. Sun Yat Sen tried to recruit revolutionaries in Japan, Qiu Jin was among the first to respond. She became one of the chief leaders of the armed rebellion against the Manchu Empire.

As director of Datong School, under the guise of physical education, she trained students for the military. During July 1907 in Zhejiang and Anhui provinces, her plan to hold simultaneous uprisings failed. After random assassins and undisciplined actions, the whole plot was exposed. To protect teachers and students of the school, she sent them home while she remained to destroy lists of names and other documents.

On July 13th, 1907, the Manchu army stormed the school and arrested her. She was tried that very night and when tortured, she wrote only one line—the last poem in the following collection—in which her name Qiu (autumn) was made into a symbol. Before her beheading at 4 a.m. two days later, she asked only for one mercy: not to strip her to the waist which all criminals to be decapitated, male or female, were subject to.

1. Autumn Rain, after My Friend Has Left

How my body flares an incense,
men and mother planting in me.
Alone, with friends my bones and flesh.
Tears, a victim of old strain and habit.
My lush part, pearl in Hades.
Leaves drying free ghosts.

Blood is raining from the sky
cry bells singing, "Girls,
girls!"

2. The Pavilion of Moon Worship

If you live long, everywhere is home:
Strangeness wearing well,
measure night by sitting until dawn.
Seize moonflowers while they sigh
wet, each.

3. To My Sworn Sister

Fingers reaching out in rain.
To catch piss is a task.
Little red bean, don't forget!

Our bed, all our fingers.

4. Poem Written on My Own Picture in Man's Suit

Shaoxing Outlaw, dare you die?
What a curse, love.

If a dolphin reasons what to do
when it hears a sound in water,
why does flesh meet so late
what my tongue knows inside?

Raising my heart into eye beyond
mirror, beyond sky,
Jin Xiong, yes, we're one.

5. The River Is All Red

Arms of firm desire
feeling volts of gifted man
whose career families could follow:
strength is living
masculine Yin.

Hand in hand sealed in blood.
All our bodies fragrant.
Sword in flower as dragon
river clouds bridging ideal.

6. Fragments

The song in breath is light and dark.

Why me, spirit?
How you push, mother!

Autumn wind and rain,
a h !

Carolyn Lau

LI-YOUNG LEE

Li-Young Lee was born in 1957 in Jakarta, Indonesia, of Chinese parents. In 1959 the family left Indonesia and, after trying to live in many countries, finally came to the United States in 1964. Li-Young Lee studied at the University of Pittsburg, University of Arizona, and State University of New York, Brockport. He won the Academy of American Poets Prize in 1979 when he was twenty-two. Since then he has won many prizes, including a National Endowment for the Arts Fellowship in 1987. His poems were collected in 1986 in *Rose*, which won acclaim by critics. Currently he is living in Chicago, working as an artist for a fashion accessories company.

I know I am not a poet. How do I know this? Because I know a poet when I read one. There are living poets in the world today. I am not one of them. But I want to be one, and I know only of one path: serious and passionate apprenticeship, which involves a strange combination of awe and argument, with the Masters.

Other than this, I don't know anything about poetry, though if space permitted, I could go on earnestly, and to the boredom and horror of everyone, about all those things I don't know.

Dreaming of Hair

Ivy ties the cellar door
in autumn, in summer morning glory
wraps the ribs of a mouse.
Love binds me to the one
whose hair I've found in my mouth,
whose sleeping head I kiss,
wondering is it death?
beauty?   this dark
star spreading in every direction from the crown of her head.

My love's hair is autumn hair, there
the sun ripens.
My fingers harvest the dark
vegetable of her body.
In the morning I remove it
from my tongue and
sleep again.

Hair spills
through my dream, sprouts
from my stomach, thickens my heart,
and tangles the brain. Hair ties the tongue dumb.
Hair ascends the tree
of my childhood—the willow
I climbed
one bare foot and hand at a time,
feeling the knuckles of the gnarled tree, hearing
my father plead from his window, *Don't fall!*

In my dream I fly
past summers and moths,
to the thistle
caught in my mother's hair, the purple one
I touched and bled for,
to myself at three, sleeping
beside her, waking with her hair in my mouth.

Along a slippery twine of her black hair
my mother ties *ko-tze* knots for me:
fish and lion heads, chrysanthemum buds, the heads
of Chinamen, black-haired and frowning.

Li-En, my brother, frowns when he sleeps.
I push back his hair, stroke his brow.
His hairline is our father's, three peaks pointing down.

What sprouts from the body
and touches the body?
What filters sunlight
and drinks moonlight?
Where have I misplaced my heart?
What stops wheels and great machines?
What tangles in the bough
and snaps the loom?

Out of the grave
my father's hair
bursts. A strand
pierces my left sole, shoots
up bone, past ribs,
to the broken heart it stitches,
then down,
swirling in the stomach, in the groin, and down,
through the right foot.

What binds me to this earth?
What remembers the dead
and grows toward them?

I'm tired of thinking.
I long to taste the world with a kiss.
I long to fly into hair with kisses and weeping,
remembering an afternoon
when, kissing my sleeping father, I saw for the first time
behind the thick swirl of his black hair,
the mole of wisdom,
a lone planet spinning slowly.

Sometimes my love is melancholy
and I hold her head in my hands.
Sometimes I recall our hair grows after death.
Then, I must grab handfuls
of her hair, and, I tell you, there
are apples, walnuts, ships sailing, ships docking, and men
taking off their boots, their hearts breaking,
not knowing
which they love more, the water, or
their women's hair, sprouting from the head, rushing toward the feet.

Li-Young Lee

Early in the Morning

While the long grain is softening
in the water, gurgling
over a low stove flame, before
the salted Winter Vegetable is sliced
for breakfast, before the birds,
my mother glides an ivory comb
through her hair, heavy
and black as calligrapher's ink.

She sits at the foot of the bed.
My father watches, listens for
the music of comb
against hair.

My mother combs,
pulls her hair back
tight, rolls it
around two fingers, pins it
in a bun to the back of her head.
For half a hundred years she has done this.
My father likes to see it like this.
He says it is kempt.

But I know
it is because of the way
my mother's hair falls
when he pulls the pins out.
Easily, like the curtains
when they untie them in the evening.

Li-Young Lee

My Indigo

It's late. I've come
to find the flower which blossoms
like a saint dying upside down.
The rose won't do, nor the iris.
I've come to find the moody one, the shy one,
downcast, grave, and isolated.
Now, blackness gathers in the grass,
and I am on my hands and knees.
What is its name?

Little sister, my indigo,
my secret, vaginal and sweet,
you unfurl yourself shamelessly
toward the ground. You burn. You live
a while in two worlds
at once.

Li-Young Lee

I Ask My Mother to Sing

She begins, and my grandmother joins her.
Mother and daughter sing like young girls.
If my father were alive, he would play
his accordian and sway like a boat.

I've never been in Peking, or the Summer Palace,
nor stood on the great Stone Boat to watch
the rain begin on Kuen Ming Lake, the picnickers
running away in the grass.

But I love to hear it sung;
how the waterlilies fill with rain until
they overturn, spilling water into water,
then rock back, and fill with more.

Both women have begun to cry.
But neither stops her song.

Li-Young Lee

Ash, Snow, or Moonlight

Tonight two step out
onto a fourth story porch,
lean against the railing, and look at the moon.
Whether they intend to stay
a while, or only a moment because something awaits,
terrible or tender,
I can't say.
Whether one mutters to the other,
or they stand in silence,
I don't know. And I don't know
if they're here together in a brief repose,
or at the edge
of something incommunicable.
I don't know
if the man shivers now because he suddenly
sees the waste his life is to be in thirty years
on another shore, or because true autumn has begun
this moment of the present year, in a province
whose name evokes in half the world
a feeling of the vastness of the world.
I can tell you there is a war
going on, but don't ask me
to distinguish if it's ash, snow, or moonlight
that creases these people's faces.

Of this man, who each night hums a song and rocks his sons.
and falls asleep before they do, his tune long gone,
his labored breathing finally lulling them,
and this woman, who sweeps by rote or moonlight
the wood floor of their one room,
what news?
They won't stay long to gaze, for the night is cold.
They look neither young nor old,
though something about the way they
stand suggests fatigue.
They will die,
and one before the other to ensure grief.
But I don't know:
is it tenderness
or habit, perhaps a tender habit,
when the woman brushes her cheek
against the man's shoulder?

Do they admire the moon's ascent, or lament its decline?
How often have I seen these two?
Am I stricken by memory or forgetfulness?
Is this the first half of the century or the last?
Is this my father's life or mine?

Li-Young Lee

Visions and Interpretations

Because this graveyard is a hill,
I must climb up to see my dead,
stopping once midway to rest
beside this tree.

It was here, between the anticipation
of exhaustion, and exhaustion,
between vale and peak,
my father came down to me

and we climbed arm in arm to the top.
He cradled the bouquet I'd brought,
and I, a good son, never mentioned his grave,
erect like a door behind him.

And it was here, one summer day, I sat down
to read an old book. When I looked up
from the noon-lit page, I saw a vision
of a world about to come, and a world about to go.

Truth is, I've not seen my father
since he died, and, no, the dead
do not walk arm in arm with me.

If I carry flowers to them, I do so without their help,
the blossoms not always bright, torch-like,
but often heavy as sodden newspaper.

Truth is, I came here with my son one day,
and we rested against this tree,
and I fell asleep, and dreamed
a dream which, upon my boy waking me, I told.
Neither of us understood.
Then we went up.

Even this is not accurate.
Let me begin again:

Between two griefs, a tree.
Between my hands, white chrysanthemums, yellow
  chrysanthemums.

The old book I finished reading
I've since read again and again.

And what was far grows near,
and what is near grows more dear,

and all of my visions and interpretations
depend on what I see,

and between my eyes is always
the rain, the migrant rain.

Li-Young Lee

RUSSELL CHARLES LEONG

It was the late Professor Kai-yu Hsu who first introduced Russell Leong's works to the American reading public in his *Asian American Authors* (1971). Since then, Leong's poems have appeared in such collections of Asian American literature as *Aiiieeeee* (1974)——under the name W. Lin, and in *We Won't Move* (1977). As the editor of *Amerasia Journal*, and the publication head of the UCLA Asian American Studies Center, Leong has been active in promoting both scholarship and literature. He is one of the co-editors, with Jean Yip, of *A History Reclaimed: An Annotated Bibliography of Chinese Language Materials on the Chinese of America* (1986) by Him Mark Lai, and the editor of *Moving the Image: Independent Asian Pacific Media Arts 1970-1990* (1991).

Fermented in the West

Dipped in salt, vinegar, sugar, alcohol, ashes, lime——I was Chinese American even before I heard the name. Growing up in Chinatown I am as much a product of it as fish or ducks or produce silhouetted against greasy windowglass. Cantonese and English syllables riddled my ears before I knew they stood for anything more.

As for writing, it was a weapon against both the romance and the lament of growing up a Chinaman in Amerika.

Living Conditions

Living under skies
hard as tendons
Among close trees
and the collective smell
of nostrils, ruts, dirt.

Living with hands
crookedly
probing for water.
Living against all eyes
that watch from
safe distances.

And turned daily
around so much
that you laugh in spite.

Russell Leong

A Race against Extinction

Over cold-white Pacific waters
under raw Spring and Autumn skies
foraging through American cities
dampened, provoked, and touched
by despair, passion, and hope

The near-extinct species
stalks idolatry
refusing to live
as parasite or prey.

Calmly
The Asian American
shatters the double myth
of Asia, interned in America
breaking through
the perception of others
to reach his own.

Russell Leong

On Shiatsu

I ask you to
"strike out the numbness
heal me with motion and quick air."

Curving both hands
You face the hawk
that rises from the chinese scroll
like a hero.

Then flattening fingers, toes, heels
you press my breath down
bluntness seeking bone.

And the pain
like a bird caught between my ribs
struggles and flies toward what is pure.

Russell Leong

Speed Writing in Amerika

Riding the bus
across Los Angeles
each passenger
alone, paired
old young dark light
holds their body close
to their clothing true
to their shoes.

So depending
upon the hour
I rush curbs
catch sweat
deflect curses
mug at cats under ladders
slice heels
on glass and tin memories.

Fragments
from the ground up
embed the future
and as for destinations
further, like china
they neither cross this bus
nor my body.

Russell Leong

Nude

Nude coil of thought
nude melon smile
casual nude
nude bar of quiet
nude cord
blinding us anyway
small nude steps
nude petal
nude grip of rock
nude green path
and red-smelling bottles
nude ear
uneven talk
nude fingers tracing
blue mud
nude laughter
of orange lips
and blazing teeth.

Nude position of
five worlds on a map
nude shining nights
nude year
sinking
nude gold cave
of your armpit
and our lives
nude to the bone.

Russell Leong

GENNY LIM

Genny Lim received her education in Journalism at Columbia University, and in Creative Writing at San Francisco State University. She has been a freelance writer/reporter, TV producer and commentator. She was a co-author of *Island: Poetry and History of Chinese Immigrants on Angel Island*, which won the 1982 American Book Award. Her play, *Paper Angels*, won the 1982 Downtown Villager Award in New York where it played at the New Federal Theatre. She adapted the play into a one-hour television drama which was presented on American Playhouse in 1985. She has taught Creative Writing at the University of California, Berkeley, and is a poetry instructor for the fine arts museums of San Francisco and on the faculty at the New College of California.

To write is one thing, but to write for life is another. It is like raising a child whom you will never see, much less own. The child might die of neglect or disease or it may even live on after you have gone—in which case, it will be no concern of yours. That is the beauty of creation. That something is left, a seed, a wing, a pebble, a sign for the next transient happening along.

You're like a dead person trying to awaken, trying to see things around you with the eyes of an infant and the wisdom of a grandmother. You are caught in the shadow like a disembodied voice. Sometimes mouthing the right words to give shape to the hidden meanings can be as satisfying as a nine-course Chinese banquet. Maybe more so.

All Blues

A flute blowing in the wind
  Fingers gliding up the
      streets of an upright bass
          tenor sax plummeting
              steep alleyways exploding
                  gray asphalt in
                  resonating blues

Hot cool
Gut blue
  Piano keys rippling over hills of
      Fuji, Kilamanjaro
          Harlem fire escapes
              cracked windows
          Hot cool
          Dark blue
        Snarling tongues
  flashing neons talk of
Solitude
  Three beats to a bar
      Rooftops stacked against the sky
          crushing the moon
              as Gabriel blows
                  locking horns with the
              King of blues
                  Singin'
                      Stretchin'
                  Bendin'
              Twistin'
                  Tremblin'
                      Shoutin'
                          Laughin'
                      Cryin'

Love is
  Fightin'
what love is
if love ain't
          All blues
          All blues

Genny Lim

A Woman's Room

Woman, a tortoise
Constant like a bowl of rice at mealtime
Resilient like the flames which cooked it
Head white as Fuji
She pushes the strands from her eyes
like floes of seasons.

Woman
holding a broom
Her universe
a room
where hangs the sun
a cleaver
cutting old grudges

Woman lying
prostrate in heat
Smelling of blood and sardines
metal rust and tofu
diapers stretched across the borders to Toisan
where she takes mental flight

A dream junkie
Youth shelved
like mango in a jar

Outside the blare of garbage trucks
Scavengers dragging huge sackcloth bundles
like heavy corpses

The buzz of an alarm
activates her consciousness
left and right and
woman rises
nude
descending the stairs

Genny Lim

Portsmouth Square

They live their lives here,
    the old men.
Every afternoon they sit
    on park benches
    like weathered statuary
reading *The Chinese Times,*
    in an ancient tongue.

They are the sojourners.
Their eyes are frothy oceans
    sucked dry by time.
Their straw limbs
    where once spun sinewy muscles
        that dredged mines
        culled crops
        and hauled rails
    are flecked with age.
They possess the grass
    with the pigeons and the children
        who do not speak to them
        or call them *Gung-Gung.**

Genny Lim

*Grandfather

Dis-appearance

Hey, I'm gonna make myself invisible
so when you pass thru
you won't know what hit you

There'll be no mirrors to score
your performance on the image scale
no dark-haired nymph to suck you into oblivion

When you look thru the ether
you'll see a hollow with
the sparks of your own eyes flickering
You'll hear me laughing, goading you

Feel my limbs, they are tendrils climbing,
taking you up in flames
But look, you'll see nothing
just the fog shifting
Your own reflection, rippling, distorting, dissolving

If I was nothing but
a spirit
an empty canvas for you to paint your penis on
you could penetrate mirrors, ignite cocktail parties
swagger thru revolving door romances
like a lost movie star

It would be so easy, so simple
to be wound like a clock
not crippled by feeling or doubt
without the need to define the moment or
caution the heart

Genny Lim

No Sister

I have no sister
Night wind took her away
Now what are these hands left to do?
These ringless fingers, frozen cones

In the silence I hear
A fury that is my own
Calling, calling
A howl scraping, tearing at the wind
Aimlessly, aimlessly
I wander through grey streets, empty alleys
Shadowed by her sigh

Yesterday I fed you coke through a straw
I spooned you cantaloupe with crushed ice
You asked me what time it was
I said everything was alright
Now they're rifling through your closet
Trying on your best clothes

These seven hills cannot contain the gulls' swoop and cry

Genny Lim

Surrender

Our flesh breathes.
Whatever flesh has passed before is dust.
My skin, riveted to yours,
smooth as glass, soft as light,
Yields like fish to the sea.
Loneliness years deep has left an empty mouth.
Now my breasts swell like anemones in your hands
And your warmth enters me.

Genny Lim

Dreadlocked

Something
a martini olive
the cream in my coffee
is missing
is always like a movie

I went to Ocean Beach
Everything was silver-chrome
The waves, the foam, the shoreline, the horizon
all shades of silver-gray
Dotted with real people, real dogs, real air
real cinema

Colette was reading lines from my play in
a monosyllabic six-year old way
My impulse was to grab it from her hands
and hide my secrets
The way my mother hid them from me and
her mother from her.
I pinch Dani's fat little cheeks because
I'm afraid those bulbous pouches will
fade like buds in a vase.
I hear her little footsteps running
away from me, becoming ladylike, knowledgeable, hesistant, afraid.
I see the dimpled elbows, ankles and knees encroached
by slim angles, coy, measured movements.
My love for them is a flowing current which I keep chasing.
I suck those budding morsels of cheeks,
my jaw widening like a fox about to swallow
the last juicy clump of summer grapes . . .
so hungry am I to devour the bloom, the moment
that she is so naturally without possession.
(I play this game so often she has come to expect and demand it.)
I pounce, *Hep, Hep!* she recoils, giggles, squeals with her
little Rubens' arms flailing in mock/terror/pleasure.
M-mumpwamph! I have gobbled her up.

The bay from my rooftop looks like a hand-tinted postcard
from the fifties, clear and aqua.
An artificial crystal reality.
Alcatraz so sharply etched you can see every black cell window
The water so blue-green you can taste its stillness

Danielle tries to hang from a low-hanging clothesline which
Paw-Paw uses to dry her *op-keen* (duck gizzards)
No! No! I yell as she skirts in and out of wet sheets, trousers,
pulling off a pair of knee socks.
She's a colt escaping my arms, my demons
Where a part of me lies buried
like a sleepwalker waiting to be roused,
freed, to taste the fire of some lost city,
smell the smoldering flesh of humanity
the fresh, rusty scent of my own womanhood,
overpowering, consuming as the sea . . .

I lie alone
Where is he?
Lonely as the sound of my own breath
My tongue wipes my thick parched lips
The tips of my breasts under my shirt look like lemons
I think the thoughts of a widow
Pitifully loyal, whispering a dead name to the wind
not wanting to awaken
I wear my love like tunnelvision
A halo bequeathed by the blood of
Gold Mountain women left behind
Bound by chaste doubt
It is unbecoming, grossly so, I think,
but what choice is there now?
How can I stop warning strange foreign men not to come near?
Screaming should they persist?
Nothing stops this memory
Nothing stops this beauty fading fast but never dying
This ache never gone

The act of improvising
means taking risks
not knowing where it takes you
there's no halfway
Parker, Coltrane, Hendrix
Blew it all out
Billie lived it
Tu Fu looked back all his life but that never kept him from going on
Understand the past but move on
Don't set yourself traps

This morning I dreamt my lips were melting
My younger daughter's lips also began melting

I had forgotten to close the microwave oven door
as I was heating her milk
I was carrying her in my arms as we both waited
When I'd realized what had happened I put my fingers to my
lips and felt their texture change from malleable flesh to
raw tissue, then I looked in the mirror and my mouth was
starting to ooze with the lower lip spreading out from the
inside like the wax of a burning candle
Then I looked at my daughter and her lower lip also began to
change and distort like that of a *Hibakushi* victim
and I was horrified, remorseful for once again
forgetting

Then I remember being in the garden of the house I lived in
when I was still married and huge, fertile branches had spread
from the pear tree, which had been my favorite tree along with
the tall palm, because I could watch the seasons change from
blossoms to fruit to barren branches all year round and the
robins or doves that had made their nests on camouflaged branches
which I could see as I cooked on my stove
They had grown so wild and dense, across the concrete path
leading to the doorway, that I had to cut the branches off
They had simply taken over the garden since the year and-a-half
I'd been gone

I kept cutting branches
trying to work myself back
to the doorway
back to the beginning
I don't remember there being an ending
as all dreams have no endings
It seems we could go on ceaselessly if we never woke up
Our lives would be a procession of images
from a backlog of other lives and images

I want to go back to
the ocean
pick up a shell, a rock, a piece of glass
and send them to you
as a reflection
as a document
as a history
as a souvenir
of a woman's life
lived
not dreamed

Genny Lim

SHIRLEY GEOK-LIN LIM

Shirley Geok-lin Lim was born in Malacca, Malaysia, to a Nonya (Malaysian assimilated) family. One of ten children, she received a Ph.D. in English and American Literature from Brandeis University in 1973. Her first book of poems, *Crossing the Peninsula*, won the 1980 Commonwealth Poetry Prize. She has published two other poetry collections and a book of short stories, *Another Country*. She is co-editor of *The Forbidden Stitch: An Asian American Women's Anthology*, which received the American Book Award of the Before Columbus Foundation in 1990.

I was schooled in the poetics of the British Empire. As a graduate student at Brandeis University, reading William Carlos Williams and Robert Creeley was my liberation praxis. My work is a constant negotiation of cultures, of unruly voices set in the rules of English/American forms. I draw steadily from my Malaysian sources: the Nanyang (overseas Chinese) community, colonized childhood, tropical land and seascapes. As an American, however, I am moving unsteadily into the new. Self-conscious re-constructions ask for: none of the same; all of difference; slackening; giving over; unease; zigzags; lightness; retracings; American space. The wit of the form for these is what I am chasing.

Modern Secrets

Last night I dreamt in Chinese.
Eating Yankee shredded wheat
I said it in English
To a friend who answered
In monosyllables:
All of which I understood.

The dream shrank to its fiction.
I had understood its end
Many years ago. The sallow child
Ate rice from its ricebowl
and hides still in the cupboard
With the china and tea-leaves.

Shirley Geok-lin Lim

To Li Poh

I read you in a stranger's tongue,
Brother whose eyes were slanted also.
But you never left to live among
Foreign devils. Seeing the rice you ate grow
In your own backyard, you stayed on narrow
Village paths. Only your mind travelled
Easily: east, north, south, and west
Compassed in observation of field
And family. All men were guests
To one who knew traditions, the best
Of race. Country man, you believed to be Chinese
No more than a condition of human history.
Yet I cannot speak your tongue with ease,
No longer from China. Your stories
Stir griefs of dispersion and find
Me in simplicity of kin.

Shirley Geok-lin Lim

Dedicated to Confucius Plaza

I live in a small house
On top of fifty other houses.
Every morning I face the East River
Where the air is cold as
On Tung Shen Mountains.
The mountains are made of loess
Brought down by the Yang-tze.
The city is a mountain
Also, made of Asia,
Europe and Africa.
They call it America.
Every morning I practice li,
Perform my wifely duties,
Watch color television,
And eat pop, crackle, snap.
It is not hard to be
An Asian-American Chinee.

Shirley Geok-lin Lim

Visiting Malacca

Some one lives in the old house:
Gold-leaf carving adorns the doors.
Black wooden stairs still stand
And wind like arms of slender women
Leading to the upper floors.
It is as I remembered,
But not itself, not empty, clean.

Some one has scrubbed the sand-
Stone squares and turned them red.
The marble yard is stained with rain,
But it has not fallen into ruin.
Weeds have not seeded the roofs nor
Cracked flowered tiles grandfather
Brought, shining in crates from China.

Someone has saved the old house.
It is no longer dark with opium
Or with children running crowded
Through passageways. The well has been capped,
The moon-windows boarded.
Something of China remains,
Although ancestral family is gone.

I dream of the old house.
The dreams leak slowly like sap
Welling from a wound: I am losing
Ability to make myself at home.
Awake, hunting for lost cousins,
I have dreamed of ruined meaning,
And am glad to find none.

Shirley Geok-lin Lim

Pantoun for Chinese Women

"At present, the phenomena of butchering, drowning and
Leaving to die female infants have been very serious."
(The People's Daily, Peking, March 3rd, 1983)

They say a child with two mouths is not good.
In the slippery wet, a hollow space,
Smooth, gumming, echoing wide for food.
No wonder my man is not here at his place.

In the slippery wet, a hollow space,
A slit narrowly sheathed within its hood.
No wonder my man is not here at his place:
He is digging for the dragon jar of soot.

That slit narrowly sheathed within its hood!
His mother, squatting, coughs by the fire's blaze
While he digs for the dragon jar of soot.
We had saved ashes for a hundred days.

His mother, squatting, coughs by the fire's blaze.
The child kicks against me mewing like a flute.
We had saved ashes for a hundred days,
Knowing, if the time came, that we would.

The child kicks against me crying like a flute
Through its two weak mouths. His mother prays
Knowing when the time comes that we would,
For broken clay is never set in glaze.

Through her two weak mouths his mother prays.
She will not pluck the rooster not serve its blood,
For broken clay is never set in glaze:
Women are made of river sand and wood.

She will not pluck the rooster nor serve its blood.
My husband frowns, pretending in his haste
Women are made of river sand and wood.
Milk soaks the bedding. I cannot bear the waste.

My husband frowns, pretending in his haste.
Oh clean the girl, dress her in ashy soot!
Milk soaks our bedding, I cannot bear the waste.
They say a child with two mouths is no good.

Shirley Geok-lin Lim

I Defy You

I defy you Wallace Stevens
to prove 'the exquisite truth.'
Your thirteen blackbirds rolled in one
continuous seamless world
bob in and out of my world
as do the black men and women
in Durban who skitter
on my tv screen. There is something else
than mere vision, mere imagination,
fat man of language. Something
than words and quiet time and cold mind,
although you have emptied your pockets
and peeked over the horizon of our desires
and turned back preferring your onanistic treasures.
The young Cambodian whose father drowned
in monsoon ocean knows
his sister's raped eyes are truth;
the hungry and dead are his 'exquisite truth,'
and you an American fiction.

Shirley Geok-lin Lim

My Father in Malaysia

My father in Malaysia
stands under a tree in China
fifteen years ago. A lichee tree
in Canton's People's Park. Mr. Wer
who is also at the Clinic
takes the picture with slightly
shaking hands. It is a frugal picture,
black and white, two inches by
two inches, sent across two oceans,
creased by crazy white lines like
a cracked egg, although for fifteen years
I have preserved it in plastic
between student visas, in a succession
of wallets, between check book
and dollar notes. He is gaunt,
he who loves oyster omelets,
long noodles, pure white of pork fat
between skin and lean. Now he counts
his white blood cells, reciting
numbers in letters home as he
recited mahjongg scores a year ago.
He will not let the Malaysian
doctor cut his throat. He writes,
Chinese medicine can also
callibrate blood-cells. I am unhoused
in yet another country.
I don't know how to write
to him. I do not have his motherland
address. I do not pick up
the black coffin telephone.
No one tells me he's dead
till he's been buried. Grief
is private, is it not?
Today I would call Canton
person-to-person. I'd say,
I've booked a ticket for you
to Sloan-Kettering. See, I have bank
accounts and dollar notes to save
your life here in another country.
Instead I write this poem.

Shirley Geok-lin Lim

Lost Name Woman

Mississippi China woman,
why do you wear blue jeans in the city?
Are you looking for the rich ghost
to buy you a ticket to the West?

San Francisco China woman,
you will drink only Coca-cola.
You stir it with a long straw,
sip ss-ss like it's a rare elixir.

Massachusetts China woman,
You've cut your hair and frizzed it.
Bangs hide your stubborn brow, eyes
shine, hurricane lamps in a storm.

Arizona China woman,
now you are in Gold Mountain Country,
you speak English like the radio,
but will it let you forget your father?

Woman with the lost name,
who will feed you when you die?

Shirley Geok-lin Lim

The Anniversary.

The world's fullness is gratefully
more than you can admit. The seams
pull taut, crotch aches, armpits peel
back odours like onion layers,
sliding pale skin on pale skin, till
the moisture streams through uterus,
pores, every way out, like smoggy
summer rain. The smells! as tarry sizzles
on blacktop, cement humidity, decayed rinds
of melons, pork butt, soggy lettuce.
You jiggle the fishbone
out of your throat, glad to be alive,
glad for blisters in the voice-box—
glad, naturally to be keeping score:
pow! take that, old socks, and you, bitch—
death! Even gulls scream as they score
above the garbage scow.
                             I take up my pen
in pleasure of breaking, which is happening
all over, in horror, in desire, whether
you insist or absent yourself. Praise
life's kisses, massive masseur,
kisses more than you can write: fullness
of words when even bad poets
have footsteps which stick through muck,
sloshing loosely, crippled feet in borrowed
galoshes: fullness of breasts,
their sugary heat dripping from eyes
of nipples, crying for the mouths of innocents,
the unspeaking gummy tongues in mouths
of dangling boys.
                       When the womb
is distended, the glimmering skin stretched
like a moon-curved canvas, a fat
sag of wind, if the tasty fish
jumps to the frying pan, who will blame
it? In the mother's smothering clasp,
the moist powder of her body, he is already
turning away: she is more than he can admit.
She is milk, tears, salt, sugar, vinegar
like opened wine, tart as lime
from the Chinese tropics, she is flesh,

what goes away, despairs, the fullness
of musings and kisses. He will know her
as infinity, victim, cannibal, cymbals,
humming high wires, air of his savoring,
rivers of nutrients, aridity. There
is no integrity in her mothering.
Instead, flow and breaking ocean,
blood, bile, freshly springing
saliva from eyes and yearning.
If I take up my pen in the anniversary
of fullness, if I remember also
another breaking, filaments forced
earthwards, plunged into the uncreated,
if I take up my pen, will I be forgiven?

Shirley Geok-lin Lim

An Immigrant

She's
afraid of
travelling,
stained
invitation cards,
piss
in the subway.
For her
highways
shake
like clog dances,
the backroads
mind
their own
business,
and sidewalks
grow
between
air-pockets.
She dances.
The landscape
of newness
underfoot
nauseates.
In her sleep
she has lost
and is
five.

Shirley Geok-lin Lim

Bukit China

Bless me, spirits, I am returning.
Stone marking my father's bones,
I light the joss. A dead land.
On noon steepness smoke ascends
Briefly. Country is important,
Is important. This knowledge I know
If it will rise with smoke, with the dead.

He did not live for my returning.
News came after burial.
I did not put on straw, black,
Gunny-sack, have not fastened
Grief on shoulder, walked mourning
Behind, pouring grief before him,
Not submitted to his heart.

This then must be enough, salt light
For nights, remembering bamboo
And bats cleared in his laughter.
My father's daughter, I pour
No brandy before memory,
But labor, constantly labor,
Bearing sunwards grave bitter smoke.

Shirley   Geok-lin-Lim

AMY LING

Amy Ling was born in Beijing, China and immigrated at age six to the United States with her parents and younger brother. She has lived in Allentown, Pennsylvania; Mexico, Missouri; Brooklyn and Queens, New York; Paris, France; Davis, California; Highland Park, New Jersey and presently resides in Washington, D.C. with her husband, Gelston Hinds, Jr. and their two children, Arthur and Catherine. She earned a Ph.D. in comparative literature from New York University and has taught at Georgetown University and at Harvard University. Jolted by the civil rights and women's movements into the realization that her own between-worlds history was worthy of literary exploration and research, she wrote these deeply personal poems, which appear in *Chinamerican Reflections*, published in 1984 by Great Raven Press. Her study of women of Chinese ancestry who write English prose, *Between Worlds: Women Writers of Chinese Ancestry*, was published by Pergamon Press.

deep emotion——joy, but more often pain——impells me to write. These poems, then, are the highs and lows of my life.

Fragile

Like well-trained ants we go our chosen way,
following a trail some dim ancestor lay
from home to tree and back again to hole
carrying our piece of leaf, life's only goal,
falling in line, antennae never still
not to lose that trail back to the hill
unaware that some sudden blue afternoon
a callous, careless sole could just as soon
as kick a stone, crush out our lives, confuse
the trail, topple our ordered home, refuse
to care about compartments for the queen,
the workers; like a flash that's barely seen
everything slowly built can quickly die
as oaks upturned by lightning from the sky
when crazed assassins shoot a president,
a singing star his life only half spent,
Atlanta's children murdered when they roam
and cancer strikes a cousin close to home.
So occupied are we, we don't intend
to think on what slight threads our lives depend.

Amy Ling

Remember*

he risked driving twenty miles through snow
falling thick as oatmeal in a car 80,000 miles old
because you wanted to try cross country skiing
and neither of you felt the cold as you smoothly
slid through snow-hushed pine groves

and he worked by himself on dinner urging you
to stretch out on the sofa when you both came back
exhausted from shopping for dishes, silverware,
eyeglasses and groceries

and he comforted you when you felt like Ruth in that
alien land of superhighways and suicides
from the window of the highrise Holiday Inn
just outside his highrise window

and he took you to "Close Encounters" when he lost
the bet about polishing shoes with a stiff bristle
brush
that he wouldn't believe wouldn't work and afterwards
you had a close encounter of the good kind yourselves

and he treated you to a cozy dinner in the plant-
filled-brass-polished-tin-ceilinged-glasslace-lamped
Cafe Phoebe's after he got that good news from school

and he encouraged you to be bold in expressing your
body's need and not just wait quietly for him to
initiate everything and was happy when you used him
up?

If you're honest, you've got to look
at the whole picture—that's what.

(Somehow they got caviar into the sardines.)

Amy Ling

* This is a companion piece to the poem "So What."

STEPHEN LIU

Stephen Shu-Ning Liu was born in 1930 in a sun-washed valley by the ancient Yangtse River. He began to publish poems and short stories when a boy in China. After graduation from Nanking University, he sailed to Taiwan in 1948, and came across to America. Once here, he began to write in English, and has published in many magazines. He studied and taught in various universities, winning his Ph.D. in English at the University of North Dakota. Since 1973 he has been teaching World Literature and Creative Writing at Clark Community College in Las Vegas. *Dream Journeys to China*, a book of his poems in English and his Chinese translations of them, was published by the New World Press in Beijing in 1982.

Poetic language should be simple and direct. Poetry is for common people, like fresh air and wholesome bread; and a poet, since he is just another human being, does not necessarily have a tattoo on his chest or a tumble-weed hairdo on his head.

I believe that a poet should work alone and leave group exercise to the football players.

My real heroes and masters are Shakespeare, Tu Fu, Li Yu, Flaubert, Pierre Loti, and above all, S. Alexandrivich Yessenin whose nostalgia for his old Russia still saddens and nourishes my soul.

A Walk with Miranda

We walk into water, under water,
in a mid-April afternoon spent swiftly
in 1977. We comb and sweep sea waves
as we move, leaving a luminous track
on salt stones. Small slugs do the same.

In the glowing wonder of a child's eye,
I talk about erosion, journeys, battles.
We see a Plesiosaur, with leathery heads
on its neck, suck blood from a baby whale.
Nothing looks more warring and grotesque
than the Tyrannosaur, whose stalk shakes
the ocean floor, whose paws leave scars
on cliffs, whose teeth crash hard bones
of Komodo dragons . . .

We don't know how the shadow of a 20-mule
wagon train passes. The salty field appears
remote, empty, immense, in Bad Water*,
and in this quivering evening my girl asks
for more tales, as if the sun would hang
still in a zodiac path, as if the wind
and the waves were harmless while we walk
with the dinosaurs, into thick green times.

Stephen Liu

*Bad Water: in Death Valley, Calif.

A Villanelle

In late September sun what did you say,
while I was eating apples from the tree,
and with the vagrant hawks I'd fly one day?

An hour to dream upon a bough I lay,
until your eager voice awaking me:
in gleaming mountain air what did you say?

Clouds gathered sampans of gold far away.
How would the elders let me go, go free,
and with the red-tail hawks I'd soar one day?

For last time in the tree I was to sway.
Come down, my son. Enough. Let apples be . . .
in yellow light of autumn did you say?

Too soon your eyes grew dry, your head ash gray.
After devouring your fruits in ecstasy,
and with the cold-eye hawks I'd flee one day?

A ride through storms, I leave you in dismay:
sea-billows roar, stars weep. I bend my knee
in dark December wind to hear you say:
What hawk could home on broken wings one day?

Stephen Liu

On Qing Ming Festival

Imagining this time of year, at the peak of spring,
in the high country of Fuling,
you see magpies graze in the cavities of sand stones,
you smell cow manure on the humps of earth,
you hear someone weep behind the aspens:
townfolks have come to the hillside carrying food
to their ancestors' spirits, burning paper money
and paper servants and adding new stones and trees
to the graves collapsed in last winter storms.

And down the valley of dark ferns you see a man,
quaintly dressed, bury his head in the moist furze,
shamelessly he sobs, crying out that his mother died
on her bones, he did not attend his father's funeral,
he has wandered dark side of the distant street,
and has no face to see the sun . . .
But could these day sleepers hear him below the grass?
Could they see him rise, wipe his eyes, shuffle down
the road and leave his unburned paper coins fluttering
whitely in the massive bushes, like butterflies?

Stephen Liu

The Encounter

Can you imagine that I, a landlord's son,
slipped away from reading Confucius, and
bathed in a sedge pond, on an evening hot
and dusty as any other.

Sitting there, among the floating greens,
a water buffalo casually looked me over:
his nostrils quickened, puffing forth mist,
his tail splashed, rippling the water's face.

The hillside was private, hidden in bearded
tamarisks, the air was stale, punctuated by
sudden dashes of grasshoppers' wings;
my mate gawked at me again, and for a moment

my eyes appeared indifferent as his,
I smelt like him, like the floating greens,
my feet, entangled with the sedge roots,
sinking deep into the oozy mud.

Stephen Liu

My Father's Martial Art

When he came home Mother said he looked
like a monk and stank of green fungus.
At the fireside he told us about life
at the monastery: his rock pillow,
his cold bath, his steel-bar lifting
and his wood-chopping. He didn't see
a woman for three winters, on Mountain O Mei.

"My Master was both light and heavy.
He skipped over treetops like a squirrel.
Once he stood on a chair, one foot tied
to a rope. We four pulled; we couldn't
move him a bit. His kicks could split
a cedar's trunk."

I saw Father break into a pumpkin
with his fingers. I saw him drop a hawk
with bamboo arrows. He rose before dawn, filled
our backyard with a harsh sound *hah, hah, hah:*
there was his Black Dragon Sweep, his Crane Stand,
his Mantis Walk, his Tiger Leap, his Cobra Coil . . .
Infrequently he taught me tricks and made me
fight the best of all the village boys.

From a busy street I brood over high cliffs
on O Mei, where my father and his Master sit:
shadows spread across their faces as the smog
between us deepens into a funeral pyre.

But don't retreat into night, my father.
Come down from the cliffs. Come
with a single Black Dragon Sweep and hush
this oncoming traffic with your *hah, hah, hah.*

Stephen Liu

WING TEK LUM

Honolulu businessman and poet. His first volume of poems, *Expounding the Doubtful Points*, was published by Bamboo Ridge Press in 1987 and won the 1988 Association for Asian American Studies Book Award in literature and a 1988 American Book Award from the Before Columbus Foundation.

Finding a File with a Familiar Name

"In life they were Yao and Shun, in death
they are rotten bones; in life they were Chieh
and Chou, in death they are rotten bones."
                              —Lieh-tzu

The date of the ID card cannot be read
but from other papers in the file
I can pin it down to 1917
when you are nineteen
and a student and newly-arrived.
The emulsion of the photograph affixed
has worn off in so many places
that your eyes and left side of your forehead,
most of your neck and right shoulder
are all splotches of white,
like what I imagine
spreading cancer might look like
under a microscope.
What is left is a faded sepia
that mostly hints of your nose and mouth,
the tie you wore, parts of your coat,
and the fuzzy shadow of your hair.

I try to squint to fill in the features
conjuring you up whole
as if this were the Shroud of Turin
or a trompe l'oeil by Dali.
But all I can see is an expression,
captured at that moment,
of a youth
probably told not to smile
and to sit erect,
looking proud and serious
facing the camera as if facing his new life
with so many hopes and dreams.

The file I found this photo in
does not contain much more:
a Chinese newspaper notice of your death,
the tracing of your headstone,
and a cemetary application filled out by my uncle.
What happened in those 27 years between

I do not know
though one card says
that you were an auto painter
and another mentions about when you died
that you lived on Maunakea Street.

There is no mention of a wife or child,
and I guess that is the reason why
each year in the spring
we are the ones to offer food at your grave
acknowledging that you are family
being a Lum and from our village
though none of my father's genealogies
ever mentions anything about you.

But for the contents of this file
the world has forgotten all about you,
as if—though it is harsh to say—
whatever you did in your full life
means not a whit to anyone anymore.
I could wonder all I want
about whether you supported Sun Yat Sen,
or what eligible young women thought of you,
or how often you chose
to sit beside the bustling docks
gazing out at the setting sun.

But I am loathe to make up memoirs
for that would seem too easy.
Better to close this file
to let you rest in peace
accepting these small facts
as all we have to remember you by.
It is not enough, it never is.
But we should be grateful for what we have.

Wing Tek Lum

I Caught Him Once

Gruff old fut
never showed it
even after Ma died
even near his own end
stomach mostly gone
except one time
I caught him
in his room
talking to his nurse
wistful
"I don't know how much longer . . . "
him just sitting there
face so pale
not moving
the nurse standing at his back
leaning over
expertly
to wipe the tears
as they welled up

Wing Tek Lum

A Moment of the Truest Horror

They held
her down, inserted a grenade by
force, pulling
the pin just
before letting go
with one
well-aimed heel to
seal her
doom. Quickly they ran
for cover.

      She kneels
there, disheveled, bruised and
bleeding, unmercifully
undazed, eyes wide,
thighs pale, voice
quavering, shrill, all hands clawing
about; the belly wrenches,
ready to give
birth, at
this moment of the truest horror.

Wing Tek Lum

Urban Love Songs

after Tzu Yeh

You stop to watch the Mandarin ducks.
The rest of us continue on to the flamingo lagoon.
I would like to ask what attracts you to them.
But my feet keep walking, I don't look back.

*   *   *

From a piece of cloth I cut out a heart.
In the laundromat it is washed and dried.
I can spend whole hours watching it toss and tumble.
I wonder if you feel the same way as I.

*   *   *

I wave as you enter; you take your seat smiling.
This same coffee shop now feels crowded.
We whisper to each other:
all eyes have noticed something's changed.

*   *   *

I've bought a new phone and an answering machine
because I know you will be calling.
Here's the number, which only you will have.
I plan to change the tape every hour on the hour.

*   *   *

Our friends are laughing.
They say we sit so close in your old Buick
it has become second nature for me
to exit on the same side as you.

*   *   *

Pinoccio's back!
Let's relive that night at the drive in
when I whispered that his nose was giving me ideas
and you got into my pants for the first time.

You drop the laundry off going to work.
I bring the bag back when I come home.
Neatly folded, your underthings are left on the bed
—I wish to respect certain cabinets as yours.

*   *   *

You shut the window rushing to your covers
complaining of the cold night.
I need fresh air, but am willing to compromise.
Let's just pull up the sash halfway, okay?

*   *   *

We hunt for photos in my parents' storeroom.
Look how young I was and full of dreams.
On the way out you brush against a cobweb.
Your flailing arms make me afraid.

*   *   *

A firetruck screams through my heart.
Douse the flames! Douse the flames!
I awake to find my pillow soaked with sweat.
For a moment I thought it was my tears.

*   *   *

You've stacked your boxes neatly by the door.
I find atop one Chinese poems I had bought for us.
Quietly I take the book out.
I resolve to tell you this after you have moved.

*   *   *

For my clogged sink I called a plumber.
When my cat got ill I took her to the vet.
My heart is broken
—I will not ask you to come to mend me.

Last night you made me so mad.
I've resolved never ever to speak to you again.
I regret having to put my foot down so.
I'm sending you a telegram to let you know.

*   *   *

One friend I know cut her hair short.
Another shaved his beard without regrets.
I would walk this city naked and bald
if ever I thought I could be free of you.

*   *   *

After you, I took up jogging.
I wore through my running shoes in no time.
One night I chucked them down into the trash chute.
See how trim I am these days!

*   *   *

Once I bought a single chrysanthemum on a stem.
We watched it blossom, red and full.
Those times now bring a smile to me
finding its brown petals as I sweep the floor.

Wing Tek Lum

Discovering You Speak Cantonese

to D. M. L., Esq.

Our discourses have been learned:
your roommate's briefs on rent control,
Alinsky and the attorney's role,
the mainland Chinamen's impressions of us Pakes.

While waiting at a reading,
I discover you too
went to Hong Kong to learn Chinese.
My immigrant wife eager to test you out
switches us out of English.

Your tones are funny;
you sometimes stop
searching for a forgotten phrase.

I catch myself talking slower,
conscious that I must not discourage
or put you down.

An eerie feeling comes over me.
Our relationship, once equal,
borders on the awkward: paternalistic airs.

I know now
how my wife feels talking to me.

Wing Tek Lum

On the First Proper Sunday of Ching Ming

We arrive at seven
   when the cemetary unlocks its long chain;
   as usual, others have shown up even earlier.

Lugging boxes of food through the rows of graves
   I remember as a child being scolded:
   never step on someone else's mound.

We lay out our dishes systematically.
   There are seven ancestors to do
   and we want to beat the crowds arriving later.

Here and there I see families tending to their own.
   A rush comes over me: we are like them.
   I feel proud, grateful for being Chinese.

Wing Tek Lum

Chinese Hot Pot

My dream of America
is like *dá bìn lòuh*
with people of all persuasions and tastes
sitting down around a common pot
chopsticks and basket scoops here and there
some cooking squid and others beef
some tofu or watercress
all in one broth
like a stew that really isn't
as each one chooses what he wishes to eat
only that the pot and fire are shared
along with the good company
and the sweet soup
spooned out at the end of the meal.

Wing Tek Lum

Harvest Festival Time

for Chiye Mori, Editor,
<u>*Manzanar Free Press*</u>

Those hard-scrabble folk in broad-brimmed
hats, blunderbusses
warm, handling fat
buckles, many women with dour, pious
faces, sitting
on benches, their backs
to the Old Country: spread before
them are pumpkin
pies, hot-
buttered corn
on the cob, all manner of
squash, stuffing and sliced turkey.
They wait
for the gaunt, brown
men—fellow colonists from across
another sea—who
one by
one straggle in. Some
bring loud
wives, beloved children.
They wear long gowns, pantaloons and
tunics of cotton
and silk, carrying to
the tables tall
pots of
rice gruel, white tripe, assorted
moon cake. A goose
would be juicier, a Chinaman
winks. Puritans smirk,
nodding to the
viscera floating in the gruel. We
eat our own food,
all
agree. They manage smiles
and dig in.

Thanksgiving, 1979

Wing Tek Lum

It's Something Our Family Has Always Done

On every trip away from these islands
on the day of departure and on the day of return
we go to the graves, all seven of them,
but for one the sum total of all of our ancestors
who died in this place we call home.

The drive to the cemetary is only five minutes long.
Stopping by a florist adds maybe ten minutes more.
Yet my wife and I on the day of our flight
are so rushed with packing and last minute chores.
Why do we still make the time to go?

The concrete road is one lane wide.
We turn around at the circle up at the top,
always to park just to the side of the large banyan tree
as the road begins its slope back down.
I turn the wheels; we now lock our car.

As if by rote, we bring anthuriums,
at least two flowers for each of our dead.
On our way we stop to pay our respects to the "Old Man"
—that first one lain here, all wind and water before him—
who watches over this graveyard, and our island home.

Approaching my grandparents, we divide up our offering,
placing their long stems into the holes filled with sand.
Squatting in front of each marble tablet,
I make it a point to read off their names in Chinese.
My hands pull out crabgrass running over stone.

I stand erect, clutching palm around fist,
swinging the air three times up and down.
My wife from the waist bows once, arms at her sides.
I manage to whisper a few phrases out loud,
conversing like my father would, as if all could hear.

We do Grandfather, Grandmother, and my parents below them.
Following the same path we always take,
we make our way through the tombstones and mounds,
skirting their concrete borders, to the other two Lums
and to our Granduncle on the Chang side.

Back up the hill, we spend a few moments by the curb
picking off black, thin burrs from our cuffs and socks.
We talk about what errands we must do next.
I glance around us at these man-made gardens,
thrust upon a slope of earth, spirit houses rising to the sky.

As I get into our car, and look out at the sea,
I am struck with the same thought as always.
We spend so little time in front of these graves
asking each in turn to protect us when we are far away.
I question them all: what good does it really do?

I have read ancient poets who parted with sorrow
from family and friends, fearing never to return.
Our oral histories celebrate brave peasants
daring oceans and the lonely beds: they looked even more
to blessings at long distance from their spirit dead.

My father, superstitious, even to the jet age,
still averred: but every little bit helps.
These sentiments I know, but I confess I do not feel.
Maybe it's for this loss that I still come here.
They are family, and I respect them so.

Wing Tek Lum

T-Bone Steak

for Ben Tong

The Chinese cut their meat before
sautéing with
vegetables cut up
the same
way, deeming those individual
portions of steak,
served American-
style, extravagant, dull,
unsociable,
and requiring too
much effort with the knife
while eating.

My father on occasion
brought home
one T-bone. *Máang fó, nyùhn
yàuh*, he cautioned:
heat
the skillet first,
the oil you pour just
before you lay
the steak on.
Delegated, I eased the full
slab on with wooden
chopsticks (forks and
other metal
objects puncture). The black
cast iron
splattered oil. My mother
usually told me to
put on
my shirt.
I lowered the
flame, and
every so often nudged
at the recessed
areas near the bone against
the pan's flat
surface. We
liked our

meat medium-rare, five
minutes to a
side at
most. At the chopping
block, I sliced off long
chunks, a half inch
thick, quickly
serving them on a platter ready
to eat, among
our other
sung, before the blood
oozed out completely.

No, it was not
Chinese, much less
American, that pink piece
sitting in my rice
bowl. It was,
simply, how our family
ate, and I
for one am grateful for
the difference.

Wing Tek Lum

LAUREEN MAR

Laureen Mar received her B.A. in English from the University of Washington in 1975, and her M.F.A. in creative writing from Columbia University in 1979. She was the Program Associate for Poets & Writers, Inc, and the Public Information Director of the New York State Council on the Arts. She returned to Seattle, Washington in 1986 and became the Public Relations Coordinator of the Seattle Art Museum, and Lecturer in Asian American Literature at the University of Washington. Laureen Mar's poetical works have appeared in many magazines and anthologies, including *Breaking Silence, The Third Woman*, and *Women Poets of the World*.

A note on the major problems I've encountered as a creative writer: making the time to write and making the money to afford that time. I'm also not as disciplined as I should be.

The Couch

*To wake up one day and find everything you
thought was true is false. You just can't
absorb it into your reality. If it happened
to me, I don't think I could survive it.*
                              Joyce Carol Oates
Why not?

No doubt
it has been moving closer to the front door
all along.
You call in a council of friends.
They point at you sitting on the arm.
Indeed, it appears
the couch has shifted its position.

When exactly was it, they ask,
you found yourself
sitting on the edge? Didn't you notice
how very uncomfortable it was?
No, you were reading a book, you explain.
That's no excuse.

What you wonder is why you bothered
to question it at all.
The couch, making its merry escape, frolics upside-
down and tilts itself in the doorway.
Soon the dishes will prepare dinner for themselves,
the dresser will do a stand-up comic routine,
and the books turn their spines away from you,

now that the bed's
turned false.

Laureen Mar

Domestic Furniture

Contrary to popular opinion, domestic furniture
is not a dining table that also washes windows.

1

Two chairs align themselves
with the table.
At first, they sit perfectly
opposite each other,
opposite themselves,
each chair a mirror.

The table pretends to arbitrate:
this is the known circumference.
But casual objects—
a vase of antheriums *his*
favorite flowers, a telephone
bill *her calls—*
obscure the surface.

One chair skids around the corner.

All right, I'll come over, she said.

2

The couch is full of cat hairs
They prowl around the couch like cats.
The couch is a teeter-totter,
the house, a sandbox.

Sit down, relax, smoke a cigarette.
All the while she feels
the white cat hairs grazing her black sweater,
the black cat hairs nuzzling her white skirt.

No, she said, *I won't.*

3

The bed has a ladder, rungs of a boat.
Sheets snap in the wind and fall slack.

It isn't far, he said.

Again,
She feels pushed to the edge
of the sink.

Laureen Mar

The Window Frames the Moon

Some nights the moon is the curve of a comb,
tumble of night held casually;
other nights, a plate broken perfectly in half,
box of night coveting the smooth edge.

The window frames the moon, places it
to the left of the world, to the right,
decides if it floats, hurtles, suspends,
glances, antagonizes, surrenders.

By eleven, the moon is as certain and fixed
as the clock on the dresser,
the chink in the wall,
the black tablecloth with silver dots of glitter.

Every night is the opportunity to rearrange the world!
With the window, I push the moon into place
as if it were a vase of flowers.
Oh, the glory of the night contained!

But there are nights the moon looms large,
so large it refuses to fit in the frame,
so large it refuses to splinter,
and when I push the moon, it pushes back

and fills my house, and I am forced to abandon
the clock and the dresser
to stand with the trees, leaves, grass,
taking my place among the small things of the world.

Laureen Mar

Wind Is the Irresistible

season. Everything succumbs,
the small red leaves. Old umbrellas.
The edge of a dress. The edge of the field
of hair as it floats from my neck.
This evening, the edge of the curtain at the window
I leave open for shock of cold.

It is the season I learn to thrive
on harsh weather. I draw my body, bare
of your hands, into the skins of other animals.
Across the country, your body lumbers
into slow hibernation. We sleep now in rain,
the season that leaves us damp.

Laureen Mar

Untitled

In this damp weather,
the dictionary swells.

This time, what will I try to keep
in order?

One dish breaks into two:

is it still a dish,
or now shards?

Rain, falling in pieces,
becomes sound,

and the lid just touches
the jar.

Did I tell you
I saw a firefly one night?

Of course, I tried to follow it.
Of course, it blinked

and disappeared.

This time, I didn't try to catch it,
the spark,

a single red pomegranate seed
in the honeycomb of night.

Laureen Mar

The Separation

Two children sit on a rock in the garden
tilting their heads in their hands.
They have dreamed escaping
the rhododendron grown large as a bear,
the maple releasing helicopter seeds.
They are debating changing
the scenery, the slant of street,
cars straining uphill, slipping down.

    At the window, their voices are lost.
    She listens to what echoes off glass—
    two bigger voices, growing in the house
    like a wind. One whirling, pitching
    into the clutter of furniture, toys;
    the other falling steadily like dust.
    In the closet, her suitcases sit,
    heavy and black.

Breathing hard, their breaths like clouds,
they heave the rock between them, struggling
again to set it down. What makes
this place seem right, still bound
by the maple and rhododendron? From here
they see the house, the mirror she stands in;
and feeling safe, they laugh
at the insects scuttling for new shelter,
the dirt blowing over the tracks.

Laureen Mar

DIANE MEI LIN MARK

Diane Mark received a B.A. in English and Asian Studies from Mills College and an M.A. in American Studies from the University of Hawaii, and did post-graduate film studies at New York University. Her books include *A Place Called Chinese America* and *Seasons of Light: The History of Chinese Christian Churches in Hawaii.* She was a founding co-producer of *Gold Mountain D.C.*, a radio program on WPFW-FM in Washington, D.C. She then became the Development Director of Asian CineVision in New York, and was an editor for the magazine *Bridge.* For her work there she was honored with the 1985 editor's award from the Coordinating Council of Literary Magazines. She is now back in her native Honolulu developing a variety of film and publication projects.

Through the years, my work has included many different types of writing—for newspapers, magazines, media productions, and books. I continue to write poetry because of the creative freedom it allows in language and expression. It is one form of writing safe from an editor's pen, where the pure voice can sing, off-key or uniquely in tune, judged on its own merit. Sometimes I feel that I am merely the vessel, hurrying to commit a poem to paper so that it can come to a life of its own. I expect that writing poetry will always be a part of my life. There are not many things that I can say that about.

Liberation

this revelation, the retreat of tide
from our shore,
slowly peeling back ocean's edge
unveiling a new world of
men and women
throwing out memorized lines
running to each other in slow motion
ringing pure
like the temple bell at twilight

We face each other
in bare knowing, blue wind
over the Pali
shooting into our veins

at dusk
expanding circles touch
and we speak
a wordless language

in dress rehearsal
night after night
I dream the revelation,
the retreat of tide from shore

Diane Mei Lin Mark

Memories of a Mentor

through my closed eyes
you glow in darkest night
silent cymbals
muffled, terrible timpani
and beyond—
    to sing a sun out of hiding
        to moonwalk on a beach
            to ride shotgun to the Rockies

what color
is thought? you
told me once

laughed about the mind being
a bargain basement
odds and ends
organized by value
thread-bare ideas somehow
good for the price
new notions
lining the aisles
while appropriate places
are found
at 10 it's crowded, noisy
at closing time
footsteps echo

the need to store winter food
now
more than over

walking on without you

so much ground to cover

how do you
move mountains?
you showed
me once

Diane Mei Lin Mark

Peace

at night she'll lead them too
making star tracks on the horizon
dancing in maile-scented breeze
singing through the darkness
by dawn they'll venture
after her in
cloud-glistening daylight
watching her sword and bough
skimming the treetops
charging the mountain
her face serene
as the blue and vast Pacific
smiling across the sky
soothing hurt
piercing negatives

Diane Mei Lin Mark

Gold Mountain

like dawn in the rainforest
vengeance of locked sounds
railroads
market place
gold

listen

Listen

after years of
battling
whitewaters upstream

it arrives

Singing!

Diane Mei Lin Mark

Suzie Wong Doesn't Live Here

Suzie Wong
doesn't live here anymore
yeah, and
Madame Butterfly
and the geisha ladies have all
gone
to
lunch (hey, they might
          be gone a very
          long
          time)

no one here
but
ourselves

          stepping on,
without downcast eyes,
without calculating dragon power,
without tight red cheongsams
  embroidered with peonies
without the
silence
that you've come to
know so well
and we,
to feel so alien with

seeing each other at last
so little needs to be explained

there is this strength

born female in Asian America,
our dreams stored years
in the backrooms
of our minds

now happening—
like sounds of flowers
bathed in noontime light
reaching righteously skyward!

Diane Mei Lin Mark

Dialectics

tania
an almost Tania
at midnight toasting
a hero of the revolution
a man who says let
justice be ours, and
lets loose the call
with bullet words
ripping the
air of the provinces
to shreds
for the very idea

remembering all those sleepless nights
those long, dreary treks to
deep caves cloaked
in states of
perpetual siege
of unrest
of mismatched variables

only to become
retuned to the other half
of reality
years later, following
long highways,
seeming serendipity
dissolve
to this pen moving
in converging circles
as you suspected
long ago
the full 360
and it's back to
you
tania
the almost Tania

Diane Mei Lin Mark

ARTHUR SZE

Arthur Sze was born in New York City in 1950. He graduated Phi Beta Kappa from the University of California at Berkeley and is the author of four books of poetry: *River River* (Lost Roads, 1987), *Dazzled* (Floating Island, 1982), *Two Ravens* (1976; Revised Edition, Tooth of Time, 1984), and *The Willow Wind* (1972; Revised Edition, Tooth of Time, 1981). His poems have appeared in over 100 publications, including: *The Paris Review*, *Chelsea*, *Harvard Magazine*, *Manoa*, and *Mother Jones*. He has given over 60 poetry readings, at such places as Brown University, Columbia University, University of Hawaii, Pomona College, and Naropa Institute. He is the recipient of a National Endowment for the Arts Creative Writing Fellowship, a New Mexico Arts Division Interdisciplinary Grant, three Witter Bynner Foundation for Poetry Grants, three NEA Writers-in-Residence Grants, and The Eisner Prize, University of California at Berkeley. Arthur Sze is also a translator of Chinese classical and modern poetry. Since 1985, he has taught at the Institute of American Indian Arts in Santa Fe, New Mexico, and is currently Director of the Creative Writing Program.

Sound Lag

His glazed lips
moved slower
than the
movement of words.
Overhead, black clouds
were poised
in the sky,
then moved on.
In the real sky
they had
no place to go.

The air cooled to zero.
I look again at myself
in the mirror.
The veins of the dark trees
outside
vibrate.
Their song is, at least,
mine, but
I am engaged elsewhere.
I extend my hand
through the glass
into the living world.

Arthur Sze

Sliding Away

Your hand rigid, curled into its final shape:
the rest of your body breathes.
The dark coals you pour on his grave
continue to breathe.
A snake slides through the
uneven grass
where it has cut a
name for
itself
by
sliding away.

Arthur Sze

The Taoist Painter

He begins with charcoal and outlines
the yellow fringes of the trees.
Then he rubs in the stumps, black
and brown, with an uneasy motion
of his thumbs. Unlike trees in the north,
he says, I have the option of season.
And he paints the leaves in the upswing
of the wind, and the swans craning their necks.
But the sunlight moving in patches
obscures and clarifies his view.
When he walks off in silence
we look at his painting and stand
astonished to see how, in chiaroscuro,
the leaves drift to their death.

Arthur Sze

Long-Distance

Speaking to you long-distance, I see you
dressed in black the night we went

home along Arroyo Tenorio. And smelled the piñon
smoke in your hair. (I like your hips,

waist, eyes.) Speaking to you long-distance,
I saw the sun go into a dark

red. And, in the river of the sky,
a slender fish, silver and transparent, leaped
and died.

Arthur Sze

The Owl

The path was purple in the dusk.
I saw an owl, perched,
on a branch.

And when the owl stirred, a fine dust
fell from its wings. I was
silent then. And felt

the owl quaver. And at dawn, waking,
the path was green in the
May light.

Arthur Sze

Listening to a Broken Radio

I

The night is
a black diamond.
I get up at 5:30 to drive to Jemez pueblo,
and pass the sign at the bank
at 6:04, temperature 37.
And brood: a canyon wren, awake, in its nest in the black pines,
and in the snow.

II

America likes
the TV news that shows you the
great winning catch in a football game.
I turn left
at the Kiska store.
And think of the peripatetic woman
who lives with all her possessions in a shopping cart,
who lives on Sixth Avenue and Eighth Street,
and who prizes and listens to her
broken radio.

Arthur Sze

The Aphrodisiac

"Power is my aphrodisiac."
Power enables him to
connect a candle-lit dinner
to the landing on the moon.
He sees a plot in the acid
content of American soil,
malice in a configuration
of palm leaf shadows.
He is obsessed with
the appearance of democracy
in a terrorized nation.
If the price of oil
is an owl claw, a nuclear
reactor is a rattlesnake
fang. He has no use
for the song of an oriole,
bright yellow wings.
He refuses to consider
a woman in a wheelchair
touching the shadow of
a sparrow, a campesino
dreaming of spring.
He revels in the instant
before a grenade explodes.

Arthur Sze

Throwing Salt on a Path

I watch you throw salt on the path,
and see abalone divers point to the sun,
discuss the waves, then throw their

gear back into the car. I watch you
collect large flakes of salt off rocks,
smell sliced ginger and fresh red

shrimp smoking over a fire. Ah,
the light of a star never stops, but travels
at the expanding edge of the universe.

A Swiss gold watch ticks and ticks;
but when you cannot hear it tick anymore,
it turns transparent in your hand.

You see the clear gold wheels
with sharp minute teeth catching each
other and making each spin.

The salt now clears a path in the snow,
expands the edges of the universe.

Arthur Sze

The Negative

A man hauling coal in the street is stilled forever.
Inside a temple, instead of light

a slow shutter lets the darkness in.
I see a rat turn a corner running from a man with a chair trying to smash it,

see people sleeping at midnight in a Wuhan street on bamboo beds,
a dead pig floating, bloated, on water.

I see a photograph of a son smiling who two years ago fell off a cliff
and his photograph is in each room of the apartment.

I meet a woman who had smallpox as a child, was abandoned by her
      mother
but who lived, now has two daughters, a son, a son-in-law;

they live in three rooms and watch a color television.
I see a man in blue work clothes whose father was a peasant

who joined the Communist party early but by the time of the Cultural
      Revolution
had risen in rank and become a target of the Red Guards.

I see a woman who tried to kill herself with an acupuncture needle
but instead hit a vital point and cured her chronic asthma.

A Chinese poet argues that the fundamental difference between East
      and West
is that in the East an individual does not believe himself

in control of his fate but yields to it.
As a negative reverses light and dark

these words are prose accounts of personal tragedy becoming metaphor,
an emulsion of silver salts sensitive to light,

laughter in the underground bomb shelter converted into a movie theater,
lovers in the Summer Palace park.

Arthur Sze

Horse Face

A man in prison is called horse face, but does nothing
when everyone in the tailor shop has sharp cold scissors;

he remembers the insult but laughs it off. Even as he
laughs, a Cattaraugus Indian welding a steel girder

turns at a yell which coincides with the laugh and slips
to his death. I open a beer; a car approaches a garage.

The door opens, a light comes on, inside rakes gleam;
a child with dysentery washes his hands in cow piss.

I find a trail of sawdust, walk in a dead killer's
hardened old shoes, and feel how difficult it is to

sense the entire danger of a moment: a horse gives birth
to a foal, power goes out in the city, a dancer

stops in the dark and listening for the noise that was scored
in the performance hears only sudden panicked yells.

Arthur Sze

The Leaves of a Dream Are the Leaves of an Onion

1

Red oak leaves rustle in the wind.
Inside a dream, you dream the leaves
scattered on dirt, and feel it
as an instance of the chance configuration

to your life. All night you feel
red horses galloping in your blood,
hear a piercing siren, and are in love
with the inexplicable. You walk

to your car, find the hazard lights
blinking: find a rust-brown knife, a trout,
a smashed violin in your hands.
And then you wake, inside the dream,

to find tangerines ripening in the silence.
You peel the leaves of the dream
as you would peel the leaves off an onion.
The layers of the dream have no core,

no essence. You find a tattoo of
a red scorpion on your body.
You simply laugh, shiver in the frost,
and step back into the world.

2

A Galapagos turtle has nothing to do
with the world of the neutrino.
The ecology of the Galapagos Islands
has nothing to do with a pair of scissors.
The cactus by the window has nothing to do
with the invention of the wheel.
The invention of the telescope
has nothing to do with a red jaguar.
No. The invention of the scissors
has everything to do with the invention of the telescope.
A map of the world has everything to do
with the cactus by the window.
The world of the quark has everything to do
with a jaguar circling in the night.
The man who sacrifices himself and throws a Molotov
cocktail at a tank has everything to do
with a sunflower that bends to the light.

3

Open a window and touch the sun,
or feel the wet maple leaves flicker in the rain.
Watch a blue crab scuttle in clear water,
or find a starfish in the dirt.
Describe the color green to the color blind,
or build a house out of pain.

The world is more than you surmise.
Take the pines, green-black, slashed by light,
etched by wind, on the island
across the riptide body of water.
Describe the thousand iridescent needles
to a blind albino Tarahumara.

In a bubble chamber, in a magnetic field,
an electron spirals and spirals in to the center,
but the world is more than such a dance:
a spiraling in to the point of origin,
a spiraling out in the form of a
wet leaf, a blue crab, or a green house.

4

The heat ripples ripple the cactus.
Crushed green glass in a parking lot
or a pile of rhinoceros bones
give off heat, though you might not notice it.

The heat of a star can be measured
under a spectrometer, but not
the heat of the mind, or the heat of Angkor Wat.
And the rubble of Angkor Wat

gives off heat; so do apricot blossoms
in the night, green fish, black bamboo,
or a fisherman fishing in the snow.
And an angstrom of shift turns the pleasure

into pain. The ice that rips the fingerprint
off your hand gives off heat;
and so does each moment of existence.
A red red leaf, disintegrating in the dirt,

burns with the heat of an acetylene flame.
And the heat rippling off
the tin roof of the adobe house
is simply the heat you see.

5

What is the secret to a Guarneri violin?
Wool dipped in an indigo bath turns bluer
when it oxidizes in the air. Marat is
changed in the minds of the living.
A shot of tequila is related to Antarctica
shrinking. A crow in a bar or red snapper on ice
is related to the twelve tone method
of composition. And what does the tuning of tympani
have to do with the smell of your hair?
To feel, at thirty, you have come this far—
to see a bell over a door as a bell
over a door, to feel the care and precision
of this violin is no mistake, nor is the
sincerity and shudder of passion by which you live.

6

Crush an apple, crush a possibility.
No single method can describe the world;
therein is the pleasure
of chaos, of leaps in the mind.
A man slumped over a desk in an attorney's office
is a parrot fish caught in a seaweed mass.
A man who turns to the conversation in a bar
is a bluefish hooked on a cigarette.
Is the desire and collapse of desire in an unemployed carpenter
the instinct of salmon to leap upstream?
The smell of eucalyptus can be incorporated
into a theory of aggression.
The pattern of interference in a hologram
replicates the apple, knife, horsetails on the table,
but misses the sense of chaos, distorts
in its singular view. Then
touch, shine, dance, sing, be, becoming, be.

Arthur Sze

NELLIE WONG

Born in the year of the Dog, Nellie Wong is the first-born daughter of an Oakland immigrant family. Active in the Freedom Socialist Party and Radical Women, her poems have appeared in many anthologies and journals, and are collected in *Dreams in Harrison Railroad Park* (1977) and *The Death of Long Steam Lady* (1986). She is co-featured in the documentary film "Mitsuye and Nellie, Asian-American Poets." She has taught writing at Mills College and Women's Studies at the University of Minnesota. A long-time secretary, she is currently administrative assistant in Affirmative Action at the University of California, San Francisco, and active member of the clericals union, AFSCME 3218.

Editors often reject work that they consider "didactic"; however, usually it's the idea they don't agree with. Some editors don't really want to hear anything except about our cultural ethnicity, or our families, thereby stereotyping us within the world of literature as well as without. In reality, writers of color write about everything—the world!

In essence, writing is a political and artistic act. Asian American writers must write, publish, and get their work criticized. Writing for me is as necessary as rising each morning.

So Near, So Far

Perhaps I shall never visit your graves.
But digging here and now
your bones glisten
in the palms of my hands.
Fact and fantasy,
they matter, the love of which
your granddaughter ponders
her Chinese name.

Nellie   Wong

My Chinese Love

My Chinese love does not climb the moongate toward heaven
nor flowers in a garden of peonies and chrysanthemums.
My Chinese love lives in the stare of a man in a coolie hat,
smiling to himself, content in the meanderings of his mind.

My Chinese love lives in the voices of my grandmothers
who don't see me, their granddaughter writing and singing
their joys and sorrows. Yet they pass me by on the streets,
chattering among themselves, keeping warm in crocheted hats,
carrying plastic yellow sacks of Chinese greens.

Though concubines and priestesses flourished during the dynasties,
they are not my only Chinese love. My Chinese love cannot be
suppressed in the inequities of the past, cannot be uplifted
only through the love poems of ancient women. My Chinese love
flourishes in the wails of women selling dried noodles,
in the small hands of their daughters who have been sold.

How American is my Chinese love? How anxious, how true?
Taxicabs and rickshas whiz through the streets of Hong Kong
as sampans drift along the Mekong while women wash
their families' clothes, greeting me as an American tourist.

My Chinese love wanders in search of dreams and memories,
of visions still unseen. My Chinese love is noisy, clacks
of mah-jongg tiles rising from basement rooms, permeates
like peanut oil from my mother's kitchen, shines in the bright eyes
of my father who growls and scares
the customers in our Great China Restaurant.

My Chinese love is my uncle whose skin yellowed from a lifetime
of opium addiction, yet who was born whole and pure.
My Chinese love is my curiosity of his young life, how he arrived
a bachelor on America's shores to bake Chinese apple pies.

My Chinese love burns. It laughs in the voices of children
sharing oranges with their neighborhood friends.
My Chinese love is a warrior. Physical death cannot swallow
it, banish it from a woman who won't rest
until she exhales the spirit
of each woman, man and child still fighting
to eat and live on this our inherited earth.

Nellie   Wong

Nellie Wong
431 Lee Street #5
Oakland, CA 94610

Unwritten Letter

Dear Irma,

Anger is difficult to hold in the palms of your hands.
Your eyes smart. They shoot daggers. Your mouth opens.
Are those tiny bullets that sling past my ears?
Are those tears in your blue, blue eyes?

I did not mean to hound you. Petty cash. Receipts.
They are symbols, and if you write on a sheet of paper
what you spent and sign your name, I will be able
to do my job. I will be able to fill out
the monthly Check Register and Cashier's Report.

You say that I treat you as if you were in kindergarten.
You, an administrative assistant, who types and files,
who writes news releases about the promotions of others,
who worries about moving to Los Angeles,
and leaving your home, your friends, in the wake
of this upheaval, this corporate earthquake.

I can swear it is my job I'm concerned about.
I can swear I mean you no harm, that everything we do
here in this company symbolizes this flowering,
this opening up of our lives.

You force a smile. Your voice shakes.
I answer: I work to survive, don't you?
We are not unalike and yet, high in this mist
the eve before the first day of summer, we smolder.
If we pause and examine our hearts during our coffee break,
we will encounter each other as workers. We may find
that the office carpets leave trails of coffee stains,
pencil sharpenings, multitude of forms and reports,
newspaper clippings, staples, staring at us
like eyes from a gothic novel.

You say you are sorry and I pause, thinking the calm
has arrived. But you storm, heading
into the sharp glass caged in my throat.

If the glass became birds, they would fly
but I remain behind my own desk, uncertain about your body,
how it behaves, how it moves like a startled cockatoo
trapped in this steel highrise.

Nellie   Wong

Reverberations

Inspired by my attendance at the National Hispanic Feminist
Conference held in San Jose, California, April 3, 1980.

It is easy, is it not   to find information about a women's conference?
                        to attend a women's conference?
                        to plunk down $35.00 to attend a National Hispanic
                           Feminist Conference?
                        to show your university card
                           and get in for $15.00 instead of $35.00?
                        to find out later through the Ad-Hoc Committee
                           that one could have gotten in for only $1.00?
                        to hear a woman say she is a conference goer
                           when the $35.00 fee prohibits the attendance
                           and lives of the poor?
                        to want to participate and talk about the issues
                           of Hispanic women when you are an Asian woman?
                        to hear the arguments of why
                           Hispanic is not a race?
                        to hear the women combine their solidarity:
                           Mujeres: Indio/Latina/Chicana/Mexicana?
                        to hear the word, "unity," to hear a Chicana
                           talk about the meaning and breath and life
                           of such a word?
                        to hear this Chicana say that you don't have
                           to be a mujer to fight for women's issues?
                        to live the fight, to resist the temptation
                           to say the struggle of mujeres are not yours
                           because you are simply an individual/a man/an
                           Anglo?
                        to honor the boycott of the Holiday Inn in San Jose
                           a boycott in effect since 1974?
                        to understand the boycott by the American Indian
                           Movement
                           for the first people, their rights to honor
                           the burial grounds of the Ohlone people?
                        to listen to some professional women say
                           that the boycott was not a relevant issue?
                        to listen to an Indian woman speak about the
                           boycott,
                           to support the right for the conference to be held?
                        to listen to young barrio women with their beliefs,
                           their community spirit, their hunger, their anger,
                           lead the struggle for their people?

to be making history when the T.V. newsmen talk
 only about the Indians' boycott of the Holiday Inn,
 to focus on the fight between peoples of color?
to know it's your right to attend a women's conference
 and to choose the issues that are the people's?
to organize a resistance to liberals who would cram down
 your hungry throat the illusions
 of how far we women have come?
to move the anger out, from self-expression to action,
 from individuality to community, from compromises
 to demands, for the right to live as women, as a people?
to give lip service to the necessity
 of networking women when some people have forgotten
 their birthplace in the upward climb
 toward social acceptance and purchased space?
 to hear that a woman can make it if she perseveres,
 by taking one class at a time, by taking
 her American dream into the classroom, the board room,
 farther away from the barrio?
to believe that a woman shouldn't feel guilty
 if she pursues her rights to an education,
 to become professional, if her man or children
 don't cooperate?
to walk away from a women's conference
 and think about the work that needs to be done?
to be a woman fighter, to sing the song of mujeres
 not knowing their language but understanding
 the spirit and necessity of the people's struggle?

                                        Nellie Wong

Give Me No Flowers

"Scouting for Nancy"
"Building for Jackie O"

"When Farah Diba came to the U.S.
as Empress of Iran, she liked to be
greeted in her room with bouquets of
white lilies, which the State Depart-
ment ordered specially from Holland at
a cost of $200 to $300 a bouquet."

"The Phillipines' Imelda Marcos
likes to be met at the airport with little
nosegays and by someone who can
curtsy, and she likes to find red roses
in her suite."

"Mr. Codus, Pat Nixon's favorite advance man,
knows what women like. He used to
scout out sunny yellow rooms (Mrs. Nixon's
favorite color) when she was traveling
and still sends her yellow roses on
birthdays and all special occasions."

"When Jacqueline Kennedy Onassis
tells friends that her architect has
brought her new house on Martha's
Vineyard in 'under budget,' she means
under $1 million."

San Francisco Chronicle
June 13, 1980

AN OPEN LETTER TO THE WOMEN OF AMERICA:

Do you, too, desire what these women have?
Do you, like them, wish to be catered to,
to know flowers as a symbol of privilege and protocol?
To sun in yellow rooms, to devour raspberry-filled donuts,
to have the rich and the powerful plan
to pillage, destroy this world for their own gain
while you, perfumed, petted, pampered, dream
of collecting castles in Spain like Jackie O?

Oh, women of America,

what do you desire   for the poor and the hopeless?
               for the silenced and the exploited?

Do you desire

the right of Israeli women to earn a decent salary?
the right of 100 Kabul schoolgirls not to be poisoned?
the right of mothers to know that a formula is defective?
the right of Navy lesbians to love one another?
the right of Ghanaian girls not to be smuggled?
                        sold?
                        to brothel-keepers
                        for $190 each?
the right of the boatwomen and boatgirls not to be raped
                        by Thai pirates
                        on the high seas?

Do you desire

the right, the right, the right

to live and breathe freely in our women's bodies
to be of use without our women's brains?

Oh, women of America,

give me no flowers

Instead give me

      the poems of Rosario Castellanos
      the Women of All Red Nations
      the young women of the barrios
      the struggle of Clara Fraser
      the stories of Ding Ling
      the passion of Lolita Lebron
      the power of Rosa Parks
      the will of sewing factory women

and finally

give me a memory, paper and a pen.

Nellie Wong

Where Is My Country?

Where is my country?
Where does it lie?

The 4th of July approaches
and I am asked for firecrackers.
Is it because of my skin color?
Surely not because
of my husband's name.

In these skyways
I dart in and out.
One store sells rich ice cream
and I pick bittersweet nuggets.

In the office someone asks me
to interpret Korean,
my own Cantonese netted
in steel, my own saliva.

Where is my country?
Where does it lie?

Tucked between boundaries
striated between dark dance floors
and whispering lanterns
smoking of indistinguishable features?

Salted in Mexico
where a policeman speaks to me in Spanish?
In the voice of a Chinese grocer
who asks if I am Filipino?

Channeled in the white businessman
who discovers that I do not sound Chinese?
Garbled in a white woman
who tells me I speak perfect English?
Webbed in another
who tells me I speak with an accent?

Where is my country?
Where does it lie?

Now the dress designers flood us
with the Chinese look,
quilting our bodies in satin
stitching our eyes with silk.

Where is my country?
Where does it lie?

Nellie Wong

When I Was Growing Up

I know now that once I longed to be white.
How? you ask.
Let me tell you the ways.

when I was growing up, people told me
I was dark and I believed my own darkness
in the mirror, in my soul, my own narrow vision.

when I was growing up, my sisters
with fair skin got praised
for their beauty and I fell
further, crushed between high walls.

when I was growing up, I read magazines
and saw movies, blonde movie stars, white skin,
sensuous lips and to be elevated, to become
a woman, a desirable woman, I began to wear
imaginary pale skin.

when I was growing up, I was proud
of my English, my grammar, my spelling,
fitting into the group of smart children,
smart Chinese children, fitting in,
belonging, getting in line.

when I was growing up and went to high school,
I discovered the rich white girls, a few yellow girls,
their imported cotton dresses, their cashmere sweaters,
their curly hair and I thought that I too should have
what these lucky girls had.

when I was growing up, I hungered
for American food, American styles
coded: *white* and even to me, a child
born of Chinese parents, being Chinese
was feeling foreign, was limiting,
was unAmerican.

when I was growing up and a white man wanted
to take me out, I thought I was special,
an exotic gardenia, anxious to fit
the stereotype of an oriental chick

    when I was growing up, I felt ashamed
    of some yellow men, their small bones,
    their frail bodies, their spitting
    on the streets, their coughing,
    their lying in sunless rooms
    shooting themselves in the arms.

when I was growing up, people would ask
if I were Filipino, Polynesian, Portuguese.
They named all colors except white, the shell
of my soul but not my rough dark skin.

    when I was growing up, I felt
    dirty. I thought that god
    made white people clean
    and no matter how much I bathed,
    I could not change, I could not shed
    my skin in the gray water.

when I was growing up, I swore
I would run away to purple mountains,
houses by the sea with nothing over
my head, with space to breathe,
uncongested with yellow people in an area
called Chinatown, in an area I later
learned was a ghetto, one of many hearts
of Asian America.

I know now that once I longed to be white.
How many more ways? you ask.
Haven't I told you enough?

Nellie Wong

Away from the Blue Swans

Away, away from the blue swans. Silver, pink?
I remember. In pairs, swimming across
a wallpaper sea in the upstairs bedroom.

Away and down a mahogany banister
out of Chinatown
where beancakes gleamed in flyspecked windows,
out of opium arms, out of men's hands,
pomade slick, caressing us with nickels and dimes.

Away, away from antlers,
dried lizards' necks,
hidden like pearls in herbalists' shelves,
women warbling Chinese songs, their voices drifting
out the hot summer air,
hanging onto men in grey felt hats
with silver dollars jangling in their pants pockets.

Crossing the boundaries
to the T&D on 11th and Broadway
past Jack's foot-long hot dogs,
smelling popcorn at the antics
of Abbott & Costello.

Arm in arm, our bravery
slung by our mother's warnings
uptown to the Paramount
all its silver and purple
and red velvet carpets
chewing spearmint
through the double feature
and returning to Chinatown
sucking preserved plums
and agreeing to lie

how we laughed at Abbott & Costello,
the Fat Man and Frankenstein
but dreaming the dance
of "Orchestra Wives"

how George Montgomery
on the life-sized screen
sealed our exodus
with his sensuous lips.

Nellie   Wong

MERLE WOO

Born to a Chinese-Korean family, Merle Woo is a socialist feminist, lesbian and unionist. She fights as a teacher, activist and poet for these causes. Her essays, stories and poems have appeared in magazines and anthologies, including *This Bridge Called My Back: Writings by Radical Women of Color, Plexus, The Haight-Ashbury Literary Journal, Asian American Journey, Breaking Silence, The Freedom Socialist,* and *Alcatraz 3.* In 1986 Radical Women Publications brought out a selection of her poems, entitled *Yellow Woman Speaks.*

Art and politics are integrally linked. Poets who write exclusively of nature and romantic love are privileged enough to let society remain as it is: radical change is not necessary, so they focus on the crescent moon and orchids.

But we poets who are outspoken as Asian Americans, women, lesbians/gays, workers, cannot separate ourselves from the reality in which we live. We are freedom fighters with words as our weapons—on the page or on the picket sign. And as we fight, we educate. We encourage our people to change the reality and to demand it all. And no amount of censorship will ever silence us.

Yellow Woman Speaks

Shadow become real; follower become leader;
    mouse turned sorcerer—

In a red sky, a darker beast lies waiting,
    her teeth, once hidden, now unsheathed swords.

Yellow woman, a revolutionary speaks:

"They have mutilated our genitals, but I will
    restore them;
I will render our shames and praise them,
Our beauties, our mothers:
Those young Chinese whores on display in barracoons;
the domestics in soiled aprons;
the miners, loggers, railroad workers
    holed up in Truckee in winters.
                I will create armies of their descendants.

And I will expose the lies and ridicule
the impotence of those who have called us
    chink
    yellow-livered
    slanted cunts
    exotic
in order to abuse and exploit us.
              And I will destroy them."

Abrasive teacher, incisive comedian,
Painted Lady, dark domestic—
Sweep minds' attics; burnish our senses;
keep house, make love, wreak vengeance.

Merle Woo

A Liŋwistek

SONG FOR MY COMRADES

You are my Tibetan Numerals,
My dear Squamish Vowels–
We are in complementary distribution
from the Atlantic to the Pacific.
Allophones of the same
Phoneme:

Freedom

Merle Woo

Poem for the Creative Writing Class,
Spring 1982

The silence in the classroom
of people I've grown to respect—
seems like so much potential here:
men and women
brown black yellow jewish white
gay and straight.

Classrooms are ugly,
cages with beautiful birds in them.
scraped, peeling walls
empty bookcases
an empty blackboard—
no ideas here.

And one window.
One writer comes in
from sitting on the sill,
three stories up.
We all want to fly
and feel the sun on the backs of our wings—

Inhale the breath
pulling in the energy of
seventeen people around me
and exhale
putting out my ideas, ideas, ideas.
We all want to fly out that window.
A breeze comes in once in a while,
we want to go out with it
to where the birds are.

To take flight
using the words
that give us wings.

What is language after all
but the touching and uplifting
one to the others:
scenes
poems

dreams
our own natural imagery:
coins
a train to El Salvador
sleeping, pregnant mothers
menacing garages/a fist pounding/voices yelling
a yogi
cops being the bowery boys
roller coasters
blood
a girl on a swing
roses
water, streams, rivers, oceans
rise. rise.

Who can keep us caged?

Merle Woo

Home Sweet Home

She was a Korean office worker in the 50's—
    Had been a domestic
    where her employers counted every single
        lambchop
    before she went home.

Home was a little oasis
    of peace and acceptance
    with a loving, protective family—

Here she was protected from outside intrusions;
    those rude shattering intrusions:
        racist remarks
        rude behavior
    being waited on last by the butcher
    late after a long, long day of work—
    where her boss makes fun of her nose,
        her eyes.

She comes home tired.
    Shuts the door behind her
    a sigh of relief—

Last weekend, she and her husband had gone away,
    "on a little vacation"
    to some mysterious place,
    used their savings
        to go "south".

She comes home tired.
    Puts dinner on the table
    As she sits down,
    her Catholic daughter says:

"I know where you went.

You went to get an abortion.

You are a murderer
    and will burn in hell."

Merle Woo

This is part of a longer poem titled "The Right to Choose"

Currents

During my lunch break, I walk in the pouring rain,
from where I work as a secretary
at Montgomery and Bush
to East/West Journal
at Grant Ave. and Washington.

Right across the street where my father was a butcher
at Sang Wo and Co.

I pass 25 banks on Montgomery in a four block walk.

I ride up to the third floor of the Empress of China building,
feeling a bit childish in my father's raincoat,
a cap and soaking corduroy pants,
to meet the friendly people of this Chinese American newspaper.

Virginia Mei has asked me for my Chinese name,
so East/West can translate the story of my case into Chinese.

But I don't know how to write my name—
I can only say it.

I have brought some calligraphy in black and red crayon,
hoping that this is it.
Long ago, my son Paul had been taught some Chinese
by his 1st grade teacher, Sue Lim.

Virginia laughs at what I brought.
It says "Good Luck" or something like that.

Then she asks me to say my name.
I say, "Woo Suk Ying."

She says, "Hm. Let me try."
So she grabs a piece of paper and begins to write.

As she does so, I remember
the three dashes here, the little box there.
She has gotten my name!
I haven't seen it in years.

"How did you know? How did you know?"

The people there tease me and say,
"Oh, she's known you for a long, long time."

Virginia says, "It was easy, that's a common girl's name.
And you said it with the right accent. Just right."

How I beamed with pleasure.
Saying it right.
My name being a common girl's name.
Like the Asian American working woman that I am.

> ("Merle" is not a common girl's name because my mother
> didn't want me to be a common girl like she was.)

East/West is translating the story of my unfair termination
into Chinese. Benjamin Chan, a translator there, says they want
    as much support
for my reinstatement as possible.
Because I am a "minority and a lady."

Yes, indeed, and a lesbian, a unionist, and social feminist.
What are the characters for these words?

Virginia says, "Here, let me write your name down on another
piece of paper for you. Don't lose it now."

As I leave, Virginia says, "Thank you for coming in all this rain."

I say, "Thank you for giving me back my name."

I kept explaining to them:
I only went to Chinese school for one year and flunked.
I said, I don't know my name because my mother is Korean.

> (Passing the buck to my mother.)

I said, Oh and I have every intention of learning Cantonese
very soon. Sure.

Always feeling I have to hide or make excuses when
I say I don't understand:

> "Gnaw emhew gong tong-wah."

Students, staff and I got mad and protested when we lost
Cantonese and Tagalog in Asian American Studies, UCB.

> Got fired because we protested.
> Got mad when we lost the bilingual ballot.
> Faster and faster losing bilingual/bicultural maintenance
> in the schools.
> College counselors telling Third World students not to
> study bilingual ed. because there's no future in it,
> no projected funding.

Jesus. And I'm still apologizing.

I prefer to walk back to work along Grant Ave.

Twice as many art and dry goods stores on Grant
than banks on Montgomery.

I can imagine a wet, poor, Asian humanity
sandwiched in between these two great historic streets.

Christmas carols are piped through every speaker.
I see young Chinese saleswomen in those empty shops,
talking to each other in Cantonese,
as they watch the rain drench Grant Avenue.

I know their long hours and low wages.

> (Me and my comrades are in the fight for the long haul.)

And I return to the office and finish typing up
an opinion and award
about an older white woman,
a long-term, conscientious, hard-working woman,
who was fired for just cause
because she had attempted to leave the company premises
with 4 pounds of scrap meat.

Merle Woo

JOHN YAU

John Yau is a poet, art critic and curator whose work has been published both in America and abroad. He is a frequent contributor to *Artforum*, a contributing editor to *Arts*, and was a contributing editor to the journal *Sulfur* (1985-90). He is the author of nine books of poetry, the most recent being *Radiant Silhouette: New & Selected Work 1974-1988*. He has taught at the Avery Graduate School of the Arts (Bard College), Pratt Institute, the School of Visual Arts, and Emerson College. He is a recipient of fellowships from the National Endowment for the Arts, the Ingram Merrill Foundation, the New York Foundation of the Arts, and received a General Electric Foundation Award and the Lavan Award from the Academy of American Poets. He lives in Manhattan.

What are the pronouns behind the "I," behind and between the "I" and its selves? Who or what is behind the pronouns? What are the voices suspended inside any one of us? What are the voices out there, speaking to the ones in here? Does their language meet any experience I might know? Do language and experience run along parallel tracks? How to get from here to there through language, by language, and in language. How to know that it is still to happen, even as it has and is. How to begin asking questions that will lead to other questions. I thought I would begin there.

Rumors

At the beginning of a street some say never ends
is a statue whose inscription says otherwise.

Some rivers remain questions, shifting
from side to side. Other questions
remain rivers, thick and muddy.
One bridge is a moth-eaten highway.
Another is a rhinestone bridge.

An architect wants to build a house
rivaling the mountains surrounding
his sleep, each turret mute as a hat.
He crosses a river to reach ground
hard enough to begin his plan. He crosses
a river the way a river crosses his sleep,
swirling with questions.

The inscription says the river flows back
into the mountain carrying the dead.
Silver coins on their eyes. Silver coins
engraved with the faces of those left behind.
On squealing streets. On pavements
rippling beneath a pyramid of glances.

At the beginning of a street some say never ends
is a river curving beneath the city, carrying
the architect to sleep. Every morning
the clouds resemble something more terrifying,
until all resemblance ends, and he wakes up
in an empty hall, alone on a river.

John Yau

Chinese Villanelle

I have been with you, and I have thought of you
Once the air was dry and drenched with light
I was like a lute filling the room with description

We watched glum clouds reject their shape
We dawdled near a fountain, and listened
I have been with you, and thought of you

Like a river worthy of its gown
And like a mountain worthy of its insolence
Why am I like a lute? left with only description

How does one cut an axe handle with an axe?
What shall I do to tell you all my thoughts
When I have been with you, and thought of you

A pelican sits on the dam, while a duck
Folds its wings again; the song does not melt
I remember you looking at me without description

Perhaps a king's business is never finished,
Though "Perhaps" implies a different beginning
I have been with you, and I have thought of you
Now I am like a lute filled with this wandering
description

John Yau

Third Variation on
Corpse and Mirror

I crossed the street
but not before
noticing the knife
poised along the moment's
throat, ready to divide
its destination into
two further choices.
In the yard beside me
two dogs played catch
with someone's head,
while a hand waved good-bye
to the body it once carried.

John Yau

Shanghai Shenanigans

The moon empties its cigarette over a row of clouds
whose windowsills tremble in the breeze

The breeze pushed my boat through a series
of telephone conversations started by perfume

Perfume splashed over the words of a nomad
who believed it was better to starve than to laugh

To laugh over the administration's most recent mishap
will make the guests stay until the party

Until the party is bundled in chatter
I will count the pearls lingering around your neck

John Yau

Late Night Movies

In a small underground laboratory the brain of a
movie actor is replaced by semiprecious stones,
each one thought to have once resided in heaven.

An archaeologist realized the inside of an ancient
mask carried a picture of satin meant only for its
dead inhabitant. A nurse walked into a hospital
and knew something was missing.

In the afternoon, rain washed away all traces
of the railroad station. A crow hid its head
under its wing. A tourist sneezed twice and
wondered if there was any truth to the legend
inscribed over the doorway of the pharmacy.

Beware the opinions of a dead movie actor,
an empty hospital and a wounded crow on a rainy
        afternoon,
a missing brain and a train station built beside a river,
a nurse carrying a photograph of heaven

In a small laboratory in heaven the semiprecious
thoughts of a movie actor are replaced by a brain.
The ancient mask realized the insides of the
archaeologist exuded a tincture of *Pisa*
meant only for its dead inhabitant.

Outside the train station the nurse wondered if
there was any truth to the legend inscribed
around the rims of her new tires. The brain
of the movie actor is carried by a tourist
from one day to the next.

In a small underground temple the wing of a crow
is replaced by semiprecious stones, each one
thought to have been a sneeze from heaven.

The nurse hid the hands of Orpheus under a painting
of a train station, whose shadows reached the river
where all legends began. A doctor realized the
doorway of the pharmacy was missing. A woman
wondered why a picture of heaven had replaced
her tires.

The movie actor's only desire was to be seen
by the dead, to be fixed in the lining
of clouds over their graves.

The archaeologist slept in a hospital with
as many windows as days in a year, and wondered
if there was any truth to the legend inscribed
on the semiprecious stones the tourist carried
across the plaza in the afternoon rain.
At times, the nurse thought the only desires
were the ones without names.

The head of Orpheus floated downriver, leaving
behind the hospital, where, as one version
of the legend claimed, the song would continue
forever in the hallways leading to the sea.

John Yau

Corpse and Mirror (III)

1
When the movie ends and the lights come on, the audience is puzzled by the sight of a corpse reclining on a velvet sofa in clothes of human hair. Each item has been carefully sewn, so that the hair resembles a white silk shirt and a three-piece wool suit flecked with gold.

On the mahogany table is a brass ashtray in the shape of a bulldog. Smoke curls from its nostrils as if it had swallowed a cigarette. An emerald butterfly glistens on his left index finger. In his bluish gray hands is a book whose pages are made of glass.

The next afternoon I drive to the outskirts of town, where there is a restaurant named after a traitor famous for his ingenious disguises. Many of its patrons think that even the name is a disguise and he still moves among us.

I have never been able to remember the plot of the movie, only the colors it traced against the arch of the bridge connecting the room's two halves together. On one side shines the movie and on the other sits the corpse. Passing back and forth between them is a conversation made of human hair.

2
When the movie ends, the lights come on. The audience is puzzled by the sight of a large oval mirror leaning awkwardly against a column, which wasn't there at the beginning of the evening's entertainment.

Scarves stop fluttering; and, one by one, hands settle nervously into laps, like birds circling the perimeters of their nests. Mouths twist beneath the receding wave of whispers, almost as if there were a place they could hide.

A reflection pierces the mirror, though the stage is empty. The men see a woman brushing her hair, while the women see a man trimming his beard.

Later, no one will be able to agree on what they saw. The memory of one event will twist around the memory of another. All that remains is the ache of trying to recall a moment, whose slanting roof of sunlight has long since fallen in. By then the mirror will have vanished and the movie will have started. This time in pieces.

John Yau

Shimmering Pediment

An overloaded circuit-lightning
Jammed the horizon, and for days
The echoes remained in my eyes.
But the brightest star is to begin
Anywhere. "Among the peonies,"
As an ancient Chinese poet wrote . . .

Near where the river pirouettes
Past the airplane graveyard
I wandered in as a child;
A fenced-in field; the broken
Fuselages and crumpled wings
Reclining, like sunbathers, in
Haphazard rows of damaged magnificence.

Actually, I never played on this knoll,
Though I think somehow I must have.
For around supper I felt compelled
To return to that silent and empty
Amphitheater, my plane spiraling
In a diminishing circle, as I flew
Parallel to where I am now standing.

John Yau

Red Fountain

When the last mirage evaporates
I will be the sole proprietor of this voice
and all its rusted machinery.
At dawn, pine green quilted clouds
glide down the mountain, dead and dying birds
stuck to their flypaper underbellies.
I have reread the instructions.
I have hidden the limelight vapors
and flowers of memory, their pulse
of sapphire tears. By tomorrow
or the day after, I will have collected
enough gasoline and lightning.
Do you remember the lipstick imprint?
Is it true he has my name
Stamped on his identity card?
The leaves are whiter this year
and another boat has capsized on the lake.
Did I tell you I delivered the letter?
Your eyes are green sometimes blue or brown.
I have mowed the lawn and fed the chickens.
The wind is spinning, but air has settled into the locks.

John Yau

Genghis Chan: Private Eye I

I was floating through a cross section
with my dusty wine glass, when she entered,
a shivering bundle of shredded starlight.
You don't need words to tell a story,
a gesture will do. These days,
we are all parasites looking for a body
to cling to. I'm nothing more than
riffraff splendor drifting past the runway.
I always keep a supply of lamprey lipstick around,
just in case. She laughed,
a slashed melody of small shrugs.
It had been raining in her left eye.
She began: a cloud or story
broken in three maybe four places,
wooden eyelids, and a scarf of human hair.
She paused: I offer you dervish bleakness
and glistening sediment. It was late
and we were getting jammed in deep.
I was on the other side, staring at
the snow covered moon pasted above the park.
A foul lump started making promises in my voice.

John Yau

Seance Music

Salt starts falling from my tongue
Will the poem arrive soon
And how will I recognize it

By the pages flying up from the brain
Says the striped man on television
Holding an audible tone in his hand

By its radiant crystal apparatus
Transmitting harmonic interferences
Through the moth-eaten glove of a doll

Salt continued falling from his tongue
As I strolled along the outer aspects of myself
Planting passionate incidentals in the mud

Someone's voice had been trapped inside a jar
And yes
The painting of the poem will arrive soon

And the man with a hamburger bun on his head
And the knight in a rusty armor swinging a mop
And the chicken who doesn't need his head to sing

And yes
The man in the prison uniform
Will leave his imprint in the air

John Yau

S. LEE YUNG

S. Lee Yung received her B.A. in Western Art History at Hunter College, New York. Artist by profession, she has been working as a free-lance illustrator and typesetter in various businesses around the New York area. In 1972-74 she was the treasurer, then the general administrator of Basement Workshop and in 1978 she returned to the Workshop as an Artist-in-Residence. Her poetic works have appeared in many magazines and anthologies including *Bridge, Contact II* and others. In 1979 she co-edited *American Born and Foreign: An Anthology of Asian American Poetry,* published by the poetry magazine *Sunbury.* During the 1980s, she has expanded her experiences from Japanese Taiko (drumming) to traveling to Morocco, the Philippines and China. Currently she enjoys the "multiculturalism" of Caribbean conga drumming and Arnis, Philippine stick fighting.

Since most artists are familiar with internal anguish over the precise selection of syntaxes to express their experiences in higher artistic forms, I won't get into it. I have concentrated on painting, photography, and writing, but the problem with my work is that much of it is taboo in mainstream publishing. We were supposed to "overcome 'our' racisms," but I still feel a frantic need to record a heritage following the inscribed walls of Angel Island.

Woman on Broadway and 95th Street

A woman screams on broadway
carrying the empty baby's chair
the cop cars comin' and people watchin'
a Black woman,
she screams in anguish
she looking at the man
Her face in contortions
twisted & screamin' pointing at him
"I'm gonna kill him"
One man holler'n
"Come here
    Get in the taxi"
she stands, then bends &
opens her mouth in anguish
No sound is emitted
but she feels
Oh—h—how it hurts
to see that empty toddler's chair
held in her hand.

How it hurts, how it hurts
to feel the needle in the womb
and extract premature flesh
How I feel, I feel,
the tears roll round the curve
of my bones
& hollow is the womb.

S. Lee Yung

Impotent Poet

(An ex-Vietnam Veteran who ran amok in C-town)

You called from Chinatown, so
    You can read your lifeless poem
      to me in Prospect Park.
I wanted to hear the
      trees rustle in the wind,
      And see the child play
        frisbee.
You had no meaning when
      you wanted to explain
      to me that yr sex
      will be a harmless ordeal.
And yr senseless
      cold wrds exhaled
      the numbed enjoyment
      found in yr purged wars,
        where dwells those timeless
        moments in yr memories.

There are things that should
      be kept untold.
When we marched to D.C.
      yr murderous mind enslaved us/
      with napalmed villages
      & deformed children
We stayed home with afflicted
      hearts barking of ghetto
      tourist traps,
      rats eating gourmet delicacies,
      the lungs of seamstresses
        filled with TB dirt,
& men gambling their fantan dreams
      in fluorescent solitudes.

So, silently I sit on this mound,
      in this park,
      & hear in the wind yr
      vomit of a war that ended
      some years ago.

Of what
            you did in a foreign land.
                        (And you wanted to explain
                        to me that yr sex
                        will be a harmless ordeal)
Citing to me those inner thoughts
            that made you go there
            so you can come back and
            rot in yr own country,
a disease that yr own
            soul will not forgive,
            and *I*
            cannot give absolution.

(Yr smell scares me).
        as you tell me of yr walking death.
        Held under fatigue covers.

                                            S. Lee Yung

Vignettes

She'd say
"Always eat in
         SILENCE"
Ne'er do or say violent
         things on Chinese
         celebrations
Even though I felt
         like yelling NO!
"Stay home & cook the meals,
do the house chores
& you'll marry someday."

Daddy was Americanized
         who fought in WWII,
         North Africa
         lik'd gamblin'
         drivin' to the countryside
         n' go fishin'.
He'd live in the attic
         with HOUSE & GARDEN
         next to his bed,
         wantin' to forget the so-called
         responsibility of three children
Just gettin' drunk
         & ramblin' on & on
         to defy racism.

Only,
once on Xmas, makin' a night visit
I heard Daddy
whistled & tiptoed
         into the house
He set two velvet boxes
         on the desk
& I stood up on my crib
"Daddy, teach me to whistle"
He told me to
"Curl your tongue
         tighten your lips
         & whistle."
He left behind
  one cameo set

the gold wrapped
round the black stone.
the other inset with a
faceted pink glass
in a fleur-de-lis shell,
sparklin' the eye.
His daughters felt like ladies
of exquisite design
but never have you heard
my whistled melody.
They argued
while watchin'
"Father Knows Best"
My eyes glued to the screen
My ears filled with their
shouts, their
decision pulling the
family   apart
screamin' of who
knows best
My tongue knotted
Just holding back
as I saw a mother and
a father hug each
other, turn &
smile at their
bubbly children &
then wave to the audience.

She left the Northwest coastline,
once matched, married &
divorced
She took her children
to New York
& she learned to
throw sadness away
she remarried.
We never mentioned the sorrow of
leaving home
because we always
ate in
SILENCE.

S. Lee Yung

Could not Hear Charlie Parker, One Day
(when WRVR, a jazz station, turned to country)

We moved once
    taming and
    riding the
    north winds
    with railroad ties
    unbounded

Saturday spring morning,
    mourning
    the loss
    & on the loose
Kenny Roger's "The Gambler"
    playing and I combing my
    washed tangled hair,
    while the kids play
    in the backyard.

The Confucian blood that no-
    body could comply
    in wisdoms unknown.

S. Lee Yung